The Best of Mr. Food®
Home Cookin' in a Hurry

"If home cookin' is what you're cravin', then look right here for homemade favorites like Mama used to make— packed with flavor but ready in half the time!"

Weeknight Spaghetti with
No-Fuss Meatballs, pages 64
and 65

Quick Greek Salad,
page 123

Easy Perfect Chocolate Cake,
page 171

The Best of **Mr. Food**®
Home Cookin' in a Hurry

Oxmoor House®

©2003 by Oxmoor House, Inc.
Book Division of Southern Progress Corporation
P.O. Box 2463, Birmingham, Alabama 35201

ISBN: 0-8487-2732-0
ISSN: 1534-5505

Printed in the United States of America
First Printing 2003

Mr. Food®, the Caricature Logo, and OOH IT'S SO GOOD!! are registered marks owned by Ginsburg Enterprises Incorporated.

Ginsburg Enterprises Incorporated
   Chief Executive Officer: Art Ginsburg
   Chief Operating Officer: Steven Ginsburg
   Vice President, Publishing: Caryl Ginsburg Fantel
   Vice President, Creative Business Development: Howard Rosenthal
   Vice President, Sales and Licensing: Thomas R. Palombo
   Director of Finance and Administration: Chester Rosenbaum

Oxmoor House, Inc.
   Editor-in-Chief: Nancy Fitzpatrick Wyatt
   Executive Editor: Susan Carlisle Payne
   Art Director: Cynthia R. Cooper
   Copy Chief: Catherine Ritter Scholl

THE BEST OF MR. FOOD® HOME COOKIN' IN A HURRY, featuring the recipes of Mr. Food, Art Ginsburg
   Editor: Kelly Hooper Troiano
   Copy Editor: Donna Baldone
   Editorial Assistant: Diane Rose
   Director, Test Kitchens: Elizabeth Tyler Luckett
   Assistant Director, Test Kitchens: Julie Christopher
   Recipe Editor: Gayle Hays Sadler
   Test Kitchens Staff: Kristi Carter, Nicole L. Faber, Kathleen Royal Phillips,
     Jan A. Smith, Elise Weis, Kelley Self Wilton
   Senior Photographer: Jim Bathie
   Senior Photo Stylist: Kay E. Clarke
   Director, Production and Distribution: Phillip Lee
   Production Coordinator: Leslie Wells Johnson
   Production Assistant: Faye Porter Bonner
   Publishing Systems Administrator: Rick Tucker

Contributors:
Designer: Rita Yerby
Indexer: Mary Ann Laurens

Cover: *Mama's Chicken Pot Pie, page 79*

Contents

Welcome!!

"In my newest cookbook, I've collected all of my favorite old-time recipes and given 'em a kitchen makeover to fit today's fast 'n' easy lifestyle. You'll find the same down-home, delicious flavor but with prep and cook times cut in half! Look for easy-to-find convenience ingredients as well as easy-to-follow, step-by-step directions. Clever kitchen tips and shortcuts are scattered throughout, making cooking easier than ever. With so many hectic schedules today, finding time with the family is even more precious, so I also share some of my secrets for making mealtimes more special. We've got you covered from party foods to main dishes to desserts and everything in between. Home cookin' has never been easier or tastier. 'OOH IT'S SO GOOD!!'"

Mr. Food

Party Hearty

*Every gathering is a
fiesta when you serve
a samplin' from these
hearty appetizers and
beverages.*

Spiced Holiday Pecans

4 cups

3   tablespoons butter, melted
3   tablespoons Worcestershire sauce
1   teaspoon salt
½   teaspoon ground red pepper
½   teaspoon ground cinnamon
Dash of hot sauce
4   cups pecan halves

1 Preheat the oven to 300°. Stir together first 6 ingredients in a bowl. Add pecans, and toss gently to coat. Place on an ungreased 10" x 15" rimmed baking sheet.

2 Bake at 300° for 25 to 28 minutes, stirring twice. Cool completely. Store in an airtight container.

"Pecan halves get a toasting and a bit of spice, courtesy of ground cinnamon, red pepper, and a dash of hot sauce. Store 'em in an airtight container to keep on hand for snackin', or package them as holiday gifts from your kitchen."

Balsamic Marinated Olives

6 cups

2   (8-ounce) jars ripe olives, drained
2   (7-ounce) jars kalamata olives,
       drained
2   (7-ounce) jars pimiento-stuffed
       olives, drained
½   cup olive oil
½   cup balsamic vinegar
1   tablespoon Italian seasoning

1 Combine all ingredients; cover and chill at least 8 hours. Let stand 30 minutes at room temperature before serving. Serve with a slotted spoon.

"Store these chunky olives in the refrigerator in an airtight container up to 2 weeks. Once your gang has devoured the olives, serve the remaining seasoned oil with salad greens—yum! You can easily cut this make-ahead recipe in half, if you'd like."

Garlic-Pepper Parmesan Crisps

8 dozen

12 ounces freshly grated Parmesan
     cheese (see tip)
2 teaspoons minced fresh garlic
1 teaspoon freshly ground pepper

1 Preheat the oven to 350°. Combine all ingredients in a small bowl, stirring well. Sprinkle cheese mixture into a 1½" round cookie cutter placed on a nonstick baking sheet. Repeat procedure with cheese mixture, placing 16 circles on 2 or more sheets.

2 Bake at 350° for 9 to 10 minutes or until golden. Cool slightly on baking sheets. Remove to wire racks to cool completely. Repeat procedure with remaining cheese mixture.

Making the Cut

Using a cookie cutter makes it easier to shape these cheese crisps into rounds but sprinkling the cheese into a free-form shape works just as well. Keep in mind, though, that your yield may change slightly. Whichever way you shape them, be sure to use only freshly grated Parmesan. Its texture plays a part in shaping these lacy crisps.

Clam Dip

3 cups

1   (10-ounce) package frozen chopped
     spinach, thawed and well drained
1   (8-ounce) package cream cheese,
     softened
1   cup mayonnaise
2   (0.9-ounce) packages dry vegetable
     soup mix
1   (10-ounce) can chopped clams

1 Combine all ingredients in a large
bowl. Cover and chill dip at least
2 hours.

2 Serve dip with bread cubes and raw
vegetables.

Clam Dippers

Take a break from the predictable chips and dip. A
16-ounce round loaf of sourdough bread that's cut into
cubes makes a hearty dipper for this appetizer. Add
some raw veggies, too—an appetizing way to get your
share of veggies!

Spicy Cheese-Beef Dip

2¼ cups

1   pound ground beef
2   green onions, sliced
1   (1¼-ounce) package taco
     seasoning mix
1   (16-ounce) jar salsa
¾   cup water

1   (8-ounce) loaf pasteurized prepared
     cheese product, cubed
¼   cup instant potato flakes

1 Cook ground beef in a large skillet, stirring until it crumbles and is no longer pink; drain. Return beef to skillet; stir in green onions and next 3 ingredients. Bring to a boil; reduce heat, and simmer 5 minutes.

2 Stir in cubed cheese until melted. Stir in potato flakes, and cook over low heat 5 minutes or until thickened. Serve warm with tortilla chips.

Make-Ahead Magic

If time is tight, prepare this dip a day ahead. Simply make it, cool it, cover it, and chill it! When you're ready to serve the dip, cook it over low heat about 15 minutes or until thoroughly heated, stirring occasionally.

Swiss-Onion Dip

4 cups

1	(10-ounce) package frozen chopped onions, thawed
3	cups (12 ounces) shredded Swiss cheese
1	cup mayonnaise or salad dressing
1	tablespoon coarse-grained Dijon mustard
⅛	teaspoon pepper

1 Preheat the oven to 325°. Drain onions on paper towels.

2 Combine onions and remaining ingredients. Spoon mixture into a 1-quart baking dish.

3 Bake at 325° for 25 minutes or until bubbly and lightly browned. Serve with large corn chips or Melba toast rounds.

"Frozen chopped onions make this dip super easy to stir up, and with 3 cups of cheese, it's guaranteed to make the top of your gang's list of favorite munchies!"

White Bean Hummus

3 cups

2   cloves garlic
1   teaspoon chopped fresh rosemary

2   (15.5-ounce) cans great Northern
      beans, rinsed and drained
3   tablespoons lemon juice
3   tablespoons tahini (see tip)
¾   teaspoon salt
¼   teaspoon ground red pepper

¼   cup olive oil

1 Process garlic and rosemary in a food processor 3 or 4 times or until minced.

2 Add beans and next 4 ingredients; process until smooth, stopping to scrape down sides.

3 Pour olive oil gradually through food chute with processor running; process until mixture is smooth. Cover and chill 1 hour. Serve with pita bread, crackers, sliced cucumber, and/or olives.

Hummus Hint
Hummus gets its distinctive flavoring from tahini, a thick paste that's made from crushed sesame seeds and is used in Middle Eastern cooking. You can find tahini in larger supermarkets and in Middle Eastern food stores.

Sweet Tortilla Triangles with Fruit Salsa

about 5 dozen

8 (8") flour tortillas
¼ cup butter, melted
6 tablespoons cinnamon-sugar

Fruit Salsa (see recipe below)

1 Preheat the oven to 450°. Brush 1 side of each of 2 tortillas with butter; sprinkle evenly with about 1½ tablespoons cinnamon-sugar. Cut into eighths, and place on baking sheets.

2 Bake at 450° for 5 minutes or until golden brown. Repeat with remaining tortillas. Serve with Fruit Salsa.

Fruit Salsa
1 cup chopped fresh pineapple
½ cup chopped fresh mango
1 cup chopped fresh strawberries
1 tablespoon chopped fresh mint
1 tablespoon lime juice

1 Toss together all ingredients. Cover fruit mixture, and chill 1 hour. Yield: 2½ cups

Savory Triangles
Try this savory variation to Sweet Tortilla Triangles. Omit cinnamon-sugar and Fruit Salsa. Brush tortillas with ¼ cup melted butter; sprinkle with ½ cup shredded Parmesan cheese, ¼ cup sesame seeds, and 1 tablespoon pepper. Proceed as directed, and serve with regular salsa.

Bacon Pleasers

2 dozen

1   pound bacon

1¾ cups (7 ounces) shredded Gouda
        cheese
1   cup mayonnaise
½   (16-ounce) package cocktail rye
        bread, lightly toasted

1 Cook bacon in a large skillet until crisp; remove bacon, and drain on paper towels. Crumble bacon.

2 Preheat the oven to 350°. Combine bacon, cheese, and mayonnaise in a large bowl. Spread mixture on rye bread slices. Place on ungreased baking sheets. Bake at 350° for 7 minutes or until cheese is bubbly. Serve warm.

"Short, simple, and scrumptious—that's the way I describe these nibbles! Only 4 ingredients, but combined, they pack plenty of first-course pleasure."

Southwestern Chicken Salad Spirals

40 appetizers

1	(7-ounce) jar roasted red bell peppers
2	cups chopped cooked chicken
1	(8-ounce) package cream cheese, softened
1	(0.4-ounce) package Ranch-style buttermilk dressing mix
¼	cup chopped ripe olives
½	small onion, diced
1	(4.5-ounce) can chopped green chilies, drained
2	tablespoons chopped fresh cilantro
½	teaspoon black pepper
8	(6") flour tortillas

1 Drain roasted peppers well, pressing between layers of paper towels; chop peppers.

2 Stir together roasted peppers, chicken, and next 7 ingredients. Cover and chill at least 2 hours.

3 Spread mixture evenly over tortillas, and roll up. Cut each roll into 5 slices, securing with wooden toothpicks, if necessary.

"Welcome friends with these zesty snacks. They're easily made ahead, so when the gang arrives, all you have to do is pull these festive bites out of the fridge for all to enjoy!"

Crab-Stuffed Peppers

16 appetizer servings

½   pound fresh crabmeat, drained and
     flaked
2   green onions, finely chopped
1   plum tomato, seeded and finely
     chopped
1   tablespoon minced fresh basil or
     parsley
½   cup mayonnaise
2   teaspoons lemon juice
½   teaspoon hot sauce

3   large red or green bell peppers
Chopped fresh basil

1 Combine first 4 ingredients in a medium bowl; stir in mayonnaise, lemon juice, and hot sauce. Cover and chill.

2 Meanwhile, cut peppers into 1½" strips. (For bite-size pieces, cut strips in half crosswise.) Spoon crab filling onto pepper strips, and top with minced basil.

"Nothin' beats the taste of fresh crabmeat, but hey, it's not always in the budget! I've found a suitable substitute that works quite well—imitation crabmeat, also called surimi. It's colored and flavored to resemble crabmeat but is actually made from a mild, white-fleshed fish. And it's a fraction of the price!"

Roasted Peppers-Feta Cheese Crostini

2 dozen

1   (8-ounce) package feta cheese
      (not crumbled)
1   (16-ounce) jar roasted red bell
      peppers, drained
1   tablespoon olive oil

1   French baguette, thinly sliced
      (see tip)

1 Preheat the oven to 325°. Cut cheese into 24 equal pieces; cut peppers into 1" strips. Wrap pepper strips around cheese pieces; secure with wooden toothpicks, and place in an 8" square baking dish. Drizzle with olive oil.

2 Bake at 325° for 20 minutes; remove toothpicks, and serve warm on bread slices.

A Base Hit

Crostini, usually served as an appetizer, features thin baguette bread slices as the base for savory toppings. A baguette is a long, thin loaf of French bread that's usually 2" to 3" in diameter. It works better than a regular loaf of French bread for appetizer-sized servings.

Pizza Snacks

8 snacks

1 (8-ounce) can crescent rolls
1 (6-ounce) package pepperoni slices
2 (1-ounce) mozzarella cheese sticks, cut into fourths
1 teaspoon Italian seasoning
¼ teaspoon garlic salt

1 Preheat the oven to 375°. Separate rolls into 8 triangles, and place on a lightly greased baking sheet. Place 2 pepperoni slices on each triangle; place 1 piece of cheese at wide end of triangle. Sprinkle with Italian seasoning. Roll up, starting at wide end. Sprinkle with garlic salt.

2 Bake at 375° for 10 to 12 minutes or until golden.

MEALTIME MATTERS

Sneak In Quality Time—Surprise the kids with an after-school snack they'll love. Squeeze in some quality time with them while they're sitting and savoring each bite by asking about their day and upcoming activities—you might be surprised by how eager they are to chat over these and other fun snacks!

Sausage and Cheese Tartlets

about 6 dozen

1 pound mild ground pork sausage

1¼ cups (5 ounces) shredded Monterey
  Jack cheese
1¼ cups (5 ounces) shredded sharp
  Cheddar cheese
1 (8-ounce) bottle Ranch-style
  dressing
1 (4½-ounce) can chopped ripe
  olives, drained
1 teaspoon ground red pepper
5 (2.1-ounce) packages frozen mini
  phyllo tart shells, thawed in
  refrigerator

1 Cook sausage in a large skillet, stirring until it crumbles and is no longer
pink; drain.

2 Preheat the oven to 350°. Combine
sausage, cheeses, and next 3 ingredients in a large bowl. Fill each shell with a
heaping teaspoon of sausage mixture,
and place on ungreased baking sheets.
Bake at 350° for 8 to 10 minutes or until
cheeses melt. Serve warm.

*"These cheese tarts may be
bite sized, but they pack a spicy
wallop—thanks to the sausage,
olives, and dressing!"*

Prosciutto-Wrapped Shrimp

8 servings

½   cup olive oil
¼   cup vermouth
2   teaspoons dried oregano
1   teaspoon pepper
6   cloves garlic, minced
16 jumbo fresh shrimp, peeled and
      deveined

8   (6") wooden skewers (see tip
      on page 110)

16 (1"x 8") slices prosciutto

1 Combine first 5 ingredients in a large heavy-duty zip-top plastic bag. Add shrimp; seal bag, and marinate in refrigerator 1 hour, turning once.

2 Meanwhile, soak wooden skewers in water to cover at least 30 minutes.

3 Preheat the oven to Broil. Remove shrimp from marinade, discarding marinade. Wrap 1 piece prosciutto around each shrimp. Thread 2 shrimp onto each skewer. Place skewers on rack of a lightly greased broiler pan. Broil 5½" from heat 7 to 9 minutes or until shrimp turn pink, turning once.

66Vermouth imparts such a distinctive flavor that I'd rather not offer a substitute, so this is an adults-only recipe, folks. Also, be careful not to marinate the shrimp too long—it'll make 'em tough.99

Caramel Hot Cocoa

4 cups

2 tablespoons sugar
2 tablespoons unsweetened cocoa
3½ cups milk
¼ cup caramel ice cream topping

1 Combine sugar and cocoa in a small saucepan; stir in milk and ice cream topping. Cook over medium heat until mixture is thoroughly heated and caramel topping dissolves, stirring constantly. Serve immediately.

"M-m-m…savor the distinct flavor of caramel in this satisfying hot cocoa. Feel free to substitute fat-free milk for regular if you're watching your waistline. You'll get the same great taste without the fat."

Speedy Spring Cooler

6 cups

1   (6-ounce) can frozen orange juice
    concentrate, thawed and undiluted
1   (12-ounce) can frozen unsweetened
    apple juice concentrate, thawed
    and undiluted
1   (1-liter) bottle club soda, chilled

1 Combine all ingredients, and serve over ice. Garnish with orange slices, if desired.

MEALTIME MATTERS

"Garnish, if Desired"—Make even the most simple food special by adding a garnish. It can be as easy as a fruit slice or sprig of parsley or as fancy as chocolate curls or tomato roses. Whichever you choose, your family and guests alike will feel special because you took extra effort in the meal preparation—and presentation!

Pineapple Fruit Punch

about 1½ gallons

1   (46-ounce) can pineapple juice
2   to 3 cups sugar
2   (2.3-ounce) packages unsweetened
      lemonade drink mix
3   quarts water
1   (12-ounce) can frozen orange juice
      concentrate, thawed and undiluted
⅓   cup lemon juice

1   (1-liter) bottle ginger ale, chilled

1 Stir together first 3 ingredients in a large container until sugar dissolves. Stir in 3 quarts water, orange juice concentrate, and lemon juice; chill 4 hours.

2 Stir in chilled ginger ale just before serving.

Ring Around the Punch

To make an ice ring, reserve 4 cups punch before chilling. Arrange assorted fruit in a 6-cup ring mold. Pour punch into mold, and freeze 8 hours. Unmold ice ring, and place in punch before serving. As the ice ring melts, it won't dilute the punch.

Rarin'-to-Go Tea

7 cups

4	cups boiling water
5	tea bags
1	cup sugar
3¼	cups cold water
1	(6-ounce) can frozen lemonade concentrate, thawed and undiluted
1	teaspoon almond extract

1 Pour boiling water over tea bags; cover and steep 5 minutes.

2 Remove tea bags from water, squeezing gently. Add sugar, stirring until sugar dissolves. Pour into a large pitcher. Add cold water and remaining ingredients; chill. Serve over ice.

❝On a hot summer day, lemonade and almond extract thrust this tea blend into thirst-quenching action! Aahh...just what the doctor ordered!❞

Easy Margarita Granita

5 cups

3	cups water
1	cup sugar
½	cup lime juice
⅓	cup lemon juice
6	tablespoons orange liqueur
6	tablespoons gold tequila
2	teaspoons grated lime rind

Additional sugar

1 Bring 3 cups water and the sugar to a boil in a medium saucepan, stirring mixture constantly. Pour into a large bowl; add lime juice and next 4 ingredients. Cover and freeze 8 hours.

2 Process frozen mixture in a blender or food processor until slushy.

3 Dip margarita glass rims into water; dip rims into additional sugar. Spoon granita into glasses.

Slush Fun
For a nonalcoholic version, omit liquors, and add ½ cup orange juice.

Cookies-and-Cream Smoothie

3 cups

2   cups cookies-and-cream ice cream
½   cup milk
1   banana, quartered
3   or 4 cream-filled chocolate
     sandwich cookies, crushed
     (optional)

1 Place first 3 ingredients in a blender; process until smooth. Pour into glasses. Sprinkle crushed chocolate cookies over each serving, if desired. Serve immediately.

MEALTIME MATTERS

Kids in the Kitchen—You'll have no problem getting help from the kids with this sweet treat. Give 'em an apron, and have 'em slice the banana, with a plastic knife of course, or operate the blender (with your supervision). And they'll get a kick out of crushing the cookies to sprinkle on top—but be sure to put the cookies in a sealed heavy-duty zip-top bag to do that! Remember, the important thing is to have fun together!

Fancy Schmancy Dinners

> **"Great-tasting, great-looking meals have never been so easy! Turn the pages to discover just the right dish for that special occasion."**

Easy Baked Lamb Chops

6 servings

1 tablespoon all-purpose flour
½ teaspoon salt
¼ teaspoon black pepper

18 (2- to 3-ounce) lamb rib chops
1 (1-ounce) package dry onion
    soup mix
1 red bell pepper, thinly sliced
1 (8-ounce) package sliced
    mushrooms
½ (14-ounce) can diced tomatoes,
    undrained
1 tablespoon steak sauce

1 Preheat the oven to 375°. Combine first 3 ingredients; set aside.

2 Tear off 1 (18" x 28") heavy-duty aluminum foil sheet. Place foil in a 9" x 13" pan.

3 Place chops in pan; sprinkle evenly with flour mixture. Top with soup mix and remaining ingredients.

4 Bring up 2 long sides of foil sheet; fold together, and then fold again. Repeat with short ends, forming a packet and leaving room for heat to circulate inside packet. Bake chops at 375° for 45 minutes.

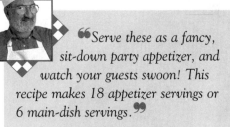

"Serve these as a fancy, sit-down party appetizer, and watch your guests swoon! This recipe makes 18 appetizer servings or 6 main-dish servings."

Gourmet Onion Burgers

4 servings

1   pound ground chuck
2   tablespoons Worcestershire sauce, divided
4   teaspoons prepared mustard, divided
1   (2.8-ounce) can French-fried onions, divided

1   (3-ounce) package cream cheese, softened
1   (2.5-ounce) jar sliced mushrooms, drained
1   teaspoon dried parsley flakes
4   kaiser rolls, toasted

1 Preheat the grill. Combine ground chuck, 1 tablespoon Worcestershire sauce, 3 teaspoons mustard, and half of onions. Shape mixture into 4 patties. Grill, uncovered, over medium heat (300° to 350°) about 15 minutes or until a meat thermometer inserted into thickest part of 1 patty registers 160°, turning patties once.

2 Meanwhile, combine cream cheese, remaining 1 tablespoon Worcestershire sauce, remaining 1 teaspoon mustard, the mushrooms, and parsley. Spread mixture on 1 side of cooked patties. Top with remaining half of onions. Serve on toasted rolls.

"Crispy French-fried onions cook inside these burgers and crown the cheesy mixture that's slathered on top after grilling. Sandwich the bounty in kaiser rolls for burgers your guests and family won't soon forget. Yum-my!"

Soy-Ginger Flank Steak

6 servings

½ cup soy sauce
2 tablespoons sesame seeds
3 tablespoons honey
3 tablespoons vegetable oil
2 green onions, sliced
1 clove garlic, minced
1 teaspoon grated fresh ginger or a
  dash of ground ginger
1 (2-pound) flank steak, trimmed

1 Combine first 7 ingredients in a shallow dish or large heavy-duty zip-top plastic bag; add flank steak. Cover dish, or seal bag, and chill 8 hours, turning occasionally.

2 Preheat the grill. Remove flank steak from marinade, discarding marinade.

3 Grill, covered, over medium-high heat (350° to 400°) 7 minutes on each side or to desired degree of doneness. Let stand 5 minutes, and cut diagonally across the grain into thin slices.

What's the Beef?

Flank steak, rump roast, and ground beef are some affordable options for flavorful family-style entrées. Watch for sales on these cuts at your supermarket, and buy extra to freeze for later. Flank steak can generally be frozen 4 to 6 months; roasts for 9 months; and ground beef 3 to 4 months.

Peppered Rib-Eye Steaks

6 servings

1 tablespoon garlic powder
1 tablespoon dried thyme
2 teaspoons ground black pepper
1½ teaspoons salt
1½ teaspoons lemon pepper
1½ teaspoons ground red pepper
1½ teaspoons dried parsley flakes
6 (1½"-thick) rib-eye steaks
3 tablespoons olive oil

1 Combine first 7 ingredients. Brush steaks with oil; rub with seasoning mixture. Cover and chill 1 hour.

2 Preheat the grill. Grill steaks, covered, over medium-high heat (350° to 400°) 6 to 8 minutes on each side or to desired degree of doneness.

MEALTIME MATTERS

No Tablecloth? No problem!—Use your noodle to think up creative alternatives to the typical tablecloth. Washable quilts, shawls, lace, fabric scraps, sheets, scarves, and even rugs make great table coverings.

Roquefort Filets Mignons with Brandy

(pictured on facing page)

4 servings

4	(6-ounce) beef tenderloin steaks (1" thick)
¼	teaspoon salt
¼	teaspoon freshly ground pepper
3	tablespoons butter
1	(14-ounce) can beef broth
¾	cup brandy
1	tablespoon chopped fresh or dried rosemary
1	cup crumbled Roquefort cheese (see tip)

1 Sprinkle steaks with salt and pepper. Melt butter in a large nonstick skillet over medium-high heat; add steaks, and cook 4 to 5 minutes on each side (medium rare) or to desired degree of doneness. Remove steaks to a serving platter; keep warm.

2 Add beef broth, brandy, and rosemary to skillet, stirring to loosen particles from bottom of pan. Bring to a boil; boil 5 to 6 minutes or until sauce is reduced to about half. Pour over steaks. Sprinkle with cheese.

66These beef tenderloin steaks are set apart with hefty doses of brandy and Roquefort cheese. Roquefort is aged blue-veined cheese that's made from sheep's milk near the French village of Roquefort. Don't worry if you don't have actual Roquefort cheese—any blue cheese will substitute. These filets will be ooh-so-good either way!99

Soft Taco Stacks,
page 80

Fried Catfish Sandwiches, page 81

Pork Tenderloin Diane

(pictured on facing page)

4 servings

1   (1-pound) pork tenderloin, cut into 10 pieces
2   teaspoons lemon pepper

2   tablespoons butter

2   tablespoons lemon juice
1   tablespoon Worcestershire sauce
1   teaspoon Dijon mustard
1   tablespoon finely chopped fresh chives or 1 teaspoon dried chives

1 Place meat between 2 sheets of heavy-duty plastic wrap, and flatten to 1" thickness, using a meat mallet or rolling pin. Sprinkle both sides of meat with lemon pepper.

2 Melt butter in a large skillet over medium-high heat. Add meat, and cook 3 to 4 minutes on each side or until done. Transfer to a serving platter, and keep warm.

3 Add lemon juice, Worcestershire sauce, and mustard to skillet; cook until thoroughly heated, stirring constantly. Pour sauce over meat, and sprinkle with chives. Serve immediately.

MEALTIME ✕ MATTERS

Music to Your Ears—A little background music can set the tone for dinnertime conversation for friends or family. For instance, pick music to reinforce an international-themed menu. Whatever you choose, keep it low enough to set the mood but still allow for quiet conversation as well as please the ages and tastes of whoever gathers 'round your table.

Garlic-Parmesan Pork Chops

4 to 6 servings

6	(½"-thick) boneless pork loin chops
½	teaspoon salt
½	teaspoon pepper
¼	cup milk
2	tablespoons Dijon mustard
1	cup Italian-seasoned breadcrumbs (prepared)
¼	cup butter, divided
1½	teaspoons prepared minced garlic (see tip)
¾	cup whipping cream
⅓	cup dry white wine or chicken broth
½	cup grated Parmesan cheese

1 Preheat the oven to 375°. Sprinkle pork chops evenly with salt and pepper.

2 Stir together milk and mustard. Dip pork chops in milk mixture; dredge in breadcrumbs. Place pork chops on a rack in a broiler pan.

3 Bake pork chops at 375° for 30 minutes or until done.

4 Melt 1 tablespoon butter in a saucepan over medium-high heat; add garlic, and sauté 2 to 3 minutes. Stir in cream, wine, and cheese; reduce heat, and simmer 3 to 4 minutes (do not boil). Whisk in remaining 3 tablespoons butter until melted. Serve over chops.

Cloves of Knowledge

Minced garlic in a jar is a flavorful way to speed up your prep time. Generally, ½ teaspoon of jarred minced garlic equals 1 medium whole clove. Jarred garlic is sold in regular and roasted varieties. (Use whichever type your recipe calls for.) Look for it in the produce section of your supermarket. Buy the jarred garlic in small quantities, and keep it in the fridge once it's opened to maximize its shelf life.

Grilled Ham and Apples

4 to 6 servings

½ cup orange marmalade
2 teaspoons butter
¼ teaspoon ground ginger

2 (½"-thick) ham slices (about 2½ pounds)
4 apples, cut into ½"-thick slices

1 Preheat the grill. Combine first 3 ingredients in a microwave-safe 1-cup glass measuring cup; microwave at HIGH 1 minute or until melted, stirring once.

2 Grill ham and apples, covered, over medium-high heat (350° to 400°), turning occasionally and basting with marmalade mixture, 20 minutes or until thoroughly heated.

MEALTIME MATTERS

Family Time Matters—Make mealtime a priority for good-quality family time. Unplug the phone, or let the answering machine take over. Encourage conversation by each person telling their favorite joke or the best part about their day. Whatever the topic, remember the important thing is that you're sitting down and spending time with your family.

BLTs with a Twist

4 servings

8	bacon slices

1	(1-pound) French bread loaf (not baguette)
¼	cup chopped fresh basil
6	ounces goat cheese
½	cup (about 3 ounces) sun-dried tomatoes in oil, drained and chopped

4	lettuce leaves
½	small red onion, thinly sliced

1 Cook bacon in a large skillet until crisp; drain on paper towels. Set aside.

2 Preheat the oven to 325°. Slice bread in half horizontally. Sprinkle basil over cut side of bottom half of loaf; crumble goat cheese over basil. Sprinkle tomatoes over goat cheese. Top with top half of loaf. Place loaf on a baking sheet; bake at 325° for 10 minutes.

3 Remove loaf from oven, and remove top half of loaf. Arrange bacon, lettuce, and onion over tomatoes; replace top half of loaf.

"The novelty behind this bacon, lettuce, and tomato sandwich is using sun-dried tomatoes, fresh basil, and goat cheese. But don't stop with basil—put your stamp on it with your favorite herb, and try different cheeses, too, like feta."

Easy Chicken Cordon Bleu

6 servings

½   teaspoon salt
¼   teaspoon pepper
6   skinned and boned chicken breast
        halves

1   (5.5-ounce) box seasoned croutons,
        crushed
⅓   cup shredded Parmesan cheese
2   egg whites
2   tablespoons water

12   thinly sliced smoked ham slices
6   Swiss cheese slices

1 Preheat the oven to 450°. Sprinkle salt and pepper evenly over chicken; set aside.

2 Combine crushed croutons and Parmesan cheese in a large zip-top plastic bag. Whisk together egg whites and 2 tablespoons water in a shallow bowl.

3 Dip chicken in egg white mixture, and drain. Place 1 breast half in bag; seal and shake to coat. Remove to a lightly greased aluminum foil-lined baking sheet, and repeat with remaining chicken.

4 Bake at 450° for 20 minutes or until chicken is done. Top each breast half with 2 ham slices and 1 Swiss cheese slice. Bake 5 more minutes or until cheese melts.

"Nobody will be singing the blues when they bite into this scrumptious entrée! With such flavorful ingredients, this dish will be a regular request from your gang— especially if you serve it with honey mustard dressing."

Lemon-Basil Chicken

4 servings

½ cup lemon juice

½ cup olive oil

½ cup chopped fresh lemon basil or basil

3 green onions, chopped

2 tablespoons white wine vinegar

½ teaspoon freshly ground pepper

4 (½"-thick) skinned and boned chicken breast halves

1 tablespoon olive oil

1 Whisk together first 6 ingredients in a large bowl, blending well. Add chicken; cover and chill 30 minutes, turning occasionally.

2 Remove chicken from marinade, reserving marinade.

3 Heat 1 tablespoon olive oil in a large skillet over medium-high heat. Add chicken, and cook 5 minutes on each side or until golden brown.

4 Strain reserved marinade into skillet. Reduce heat to medium-low, cover, and simmer 8 to 10 minutes or until chicken is cooked through and juices run clear. Serve chicken over warm cooked rice, if desired.

Basil Basics

Lemon basil looks like regular basil, but you'll recognize it by its distinct citrus aroma and flavor. Substitute here with regular basil, if desired.

Pecan Chicken

6 servings

1½ cups finely chopped pecans
½   cup fine, dry breadcrumbs
       (prepared)
½   teaspoon chopped fresh parsley or
       ⅛ teaspoon dried parsley
¼   teaspoon salt
⅛   teaspoon ground red pepper

6   (6-ounce) skinned and boned
       chicken breast halves
3   tablespoons butter, melted and
       divided

2   tablespoons vegetable oil, divided

1 Stir together first 5 ingredients in a small bowl.

2 Brush chicken with 1 tablespoon melted butter. Dredge chicken in pecan mixture, pressing gently to coat.

3 Preheat the oven to 350°. Heat 1 tablespoon butter and 1 tablespoon oil in a large skillet over medium-high heat until hot. Add 3 chicken breast halves, and cook 2 minutes on each side or until browned. Remove chicken to an ungreased baking sheet. Wipe skillet clean with a paper towel. Repeat procedure with remaining butter, oil, and chicken breast halves.

4 Bake at 350° for 15 to 17 minutes or until done.

“Some say pih-KAHN, others say PEE-kan. Either way you say it, I bet you'll love the rich, buttery flavor the pecans add to this crunchy chicken topping. If the chicken breast halves vary in size, adjust your cooking time up or down to accommodate.”

Herbed Chicken and Veggies

4 servings

¼   cup fine, dry breadcrumbs
     (prepared)
6   tablespoons shredded Parmesan
     cheese, divided
4   skinned and boned chicken breast
     halves

2   tablespoons olive oil

10 large mushrooms, quartered
1   large green bell pepper, thinly sliced
3   large tomatoes, coarsely chopped
1   large clove garlic, pressed
½   teaspoon salt
1   teaspoon dried oregano

1 Combine breadcrumbs and 4 tablespoons Parmesan cheese; dredge chicken in mixture.

2 Heat olive oil in a large skillet over medium-high heat. Add chicken, and cook 4 minutes on each side or until browned. Remove chicken from skillet.

3 Add mushrooms and bell pepper to skillet; sauté 3 minutes. Add tomatoes, garlic, and salt; return chicken to skillet. Cover, reduce heat, and simmer 10 minutes. Stir in oregano and remaining 2 tablespoons Parmesan cheese. Serve immediately.

❝To make this a complete one-dish meal, serve the chicken over rice or linguine—it's that easy!❞

Chicken in Tomato-Basil Cream

6 servings

1 tablespoon butter, melted
½ cup finely chopped onion
1 (16-ounce) can whole tomatoes,
  coarsely chopped
½ cup heavy whipping cream
½ cup chopped fresh basil
1 teaspoon salt
½ teaspoon freshly ground pepper

6 skinned and boned chicken breast
  halves

1 Melt butter in a large skillet over medium heat. Add onion, and cook 5 minutes or until onion is tender. Increase heat to high, and add chopped tomatoes; cook until liquid is almost absorbed. Add whipping cream, and cook until slightly thickened. Remove sauce from heat; add basil, salt, and pepper.

2 Preheat the oven to 450°. Place chicken in a 7" x 11" baking dish; pour sauce over chicken. Bake, uncovered, at 450° for 16 to 20 minutes or until done.

"Okay, Italian-food afficionados, this recipe is a must-try. Serve it with buttered penne pasta and hot garlic bread to top off this quick and easy dish."

Chicken Caesar Pasta

2 to 3 servings

1   (8-ounce) bottle Caesar dressing, divided
2   skinned and boned chicken breast halves, thinly sliced

2   green onions, thinly sliced
1   (10-ounce) package frozen sugar snap peas
1   carrot, peeled and thinly sliced (see tip)

1   cup torn fresh spinach
8   ounces bow tie pasta, cooked

1 Heat 3 tablespoons Caesar dressing in a large skillet over medium-high heat. Add chicken, and sauté 4 to 5 minutes or until almost done.

2 Add green onions, peas, and carrot; cook 4 to 5 minutes or until carrot is crisp-tender, stirring occasionally.

3 Add spinach; cook 1 to 2 minutes or until wilted, stirring occasionally. Toss with pasta, and serve with remaining Caesar dressing.

66Shredded carrots are readily available prepackaged in the produce department of your supermarket. Feel free to substitute 1 cup of shredded carrots for 1 whole carrot. Just add the quicker cooking shredded carrots with the spinach instead of with the green onions and peas.99

Spicy Chicken 'n' Pasta

4 servings

3	tablespoons olive oil
3	celery ribs, chopped
2	cloves garlic, minced
1	medium onion, chopped
1	green bell pepper, chopped
1	pound skinned and boned chicken breast halves, cubed
1	(16-ounce) jar medium salsa (see tip)
½	teaspoon salt
8	ounces penne pasta, cooked

1 Heat olive oil in a large saucepan over medium-high heat. Add celery and next 3 ingredients, and sauté 3 to 4 minutes or until vegetables are crisp-tender.

2 Add chicken, and cook 3 to 4 minutes or until done, stirring often.

3 Stir in salsa and salt; bring to a boil. Reduce heat, and simmer 2 minutes or until thickened, stirring often. Serve over penne pasta.

"Shake up your supper lineup with my Spicy Chicken 'n' Pasta. If you want to make it tongue-tingling spicy, use hot salsa instead."

Turkey Cutlets Française

2 servings

¾ pound turkey cutlets

1 large egg
1 tablespoon water
2 tablespoons grated Parmesan
    cheese
⅓ cup all-purpose flour
½ teaspoon salt
¼ teaspoon ground white pepper

2 tablespoons butter, divided

¼ cup lemon juice
2 tablespoons chopped fresh parsley

1 Pat turkey cutlets dry with paper towels.

2 Combine egg and water; beat well. Stir in Parmesan cheese. Combine flour, salt, and pepper. Dip cutlets in egg mixture; dredge in flour mixture.

3 Heat 1 tablespoon butter in a large skillet over medium-high heat. Add half the cutlets; sauté 2 minutes on each side or until lightly browned. Transfer to a serving platter; keep warm. Repeat procedure with remaining butter and cutlets.

4 Add lemon juice to skillet; deglaze skillet by scraping particles that cling to bottom. Pour sauce over cutlets. Sprinkle with chopped parsley.

MEALTIME ✕ MATTERS

Love is in the Air!—Proclaim your love for that special someone with a romantic feast. To create ambience, turn the lights down, light some candles, and add soft background music. I suggest pairing Easy Baked Risotto (page 94) with these succulent turkey cutlets. End the feast with a luscious finale of Chocolate Pots de Crème (page 166) and a special champagne toast.

Oven-"Fried" Halibut

4 servings

½ cup fine, dry breadcrumbs
   (prepared)
½ teaspoon lemon pepper
½ teaspoon garlic salt
½ teaspoon paprika
¼ teaspoon dried parsley

4 (6-ounce) halibut fillets
½ cup milk

2 tablespoons butter, melted
Lemon wedges

1 Preheat the oven to 500°. Stir together first 5 ingredients in a small bowl.

2 Dip fillets in milk, and dredge in breadcrumb mixture, turning to coat completely.

3 Lightly coat a 10" x 15" rimmed baking sheet with oil; heat pan at 500° for 3 minutes or until pan is very hot. Carefully arrange fillets on hot pan, and drizzle with melted butter. Bake fillets at 500° for 7 to 8 minutes or until fish flakes easily with a fork. Serve fillets with lemon wedges.

Oven-"Fried" Goodness
A coating of crisp, dry breadcrumbs and quick baking at high heat on a preheated pan make this oven-"fried" halibut extra crispy—and extra good!

Salmon with Mahogany Sauce

4 servings

2   pounds salmon fillets (1" thick)

1   cup canned whole-berry cranberry
          sauce
¼   cup honey
¼   cup soy sauce
2   cloves garlic, minced
¼   teaspoon pepper

Chopped fresh parsley

"My distinctive sauce gets its mahogany color and delectable flavor from a blending of whole-berry cranberry sauce, soy sauce, honey, and garlic."

1 Preheat the oven to 375°. Remove and discard skin from salmon; place salmon in a lightly greased 9" x 13" baking dish.

2 Stir together cranberry sauce and next 4 ingredients in a small bowl. Pour half of sauce (about ¾ cup) over salmon, spreading to coat. Reserve remaining sauce.

3 Bake, uncovered, at 375° for 20 to 25 minutes or until fish flakes easily with a fork.

4 Cook reserved sauce in a saucepan over medium heat until thoroughly heated. Serve with salmon. Sprinkle salmon with parsley.

Grilled Tuna Steaks

4 servings

1   cup water
1   cup soy sauce
½   cup vegetable oil
1   (0.7-ounce) package Italian
        dressing mix
4   (1"-thick) tuna steaks (about
        2½ pounds)

1 Combine first 4 ingredients in a large heavy-duty zip-top plastic bag; add tuna. Seal bag, and chill 1 hour, turning occasionally.

2 Spray cold grill rack with nonstick cooking spray; preheat the grill to medium-high heat (350° to 400°). Remove tuna from marinade, discarding marinade.

3 Place tuna on rack; grill, covered, about 5 minutes on each side or until fish flakes easily with a fork.

"You can't beat the simplicity or the boost that Italian dressing mix and soy sauce give to the flavor of these easy grilled tuna steaks."

Shrimp with Artichokes

3 to 4 servings

½ cup butter
1 (0.6-ounce) package zesty Italian
    dressing mix

1 (8-ounce) package sliced fresh
    mushrooms
1 (6½-ounce) jar marinated artichoke
    hearts, undrained
12 ounces peeled, deveined large fresh
    shrimp

Warm cooked fettuccine

1 Melt butter in a large skillet over medium heat; add dressing mix, and stir until dressing dissolves.

2 Add mushrooms and artichoke hearts, and cook 3 to 5 minutes or until mushrooms are tender. Add shrimp; cook 4 to 5 minutes or until shrimp turn pink.

3 Pour shrimp mixture over warm cooked pasta, and toss well. Serve immediately.

MEALTIME MATTERS

Simple Centerpiece—For an attractive and simple centerpiece, float a votive candle in a pretty crystal bowl. Fill your bowl half full with water, and add the candle. Try floating flowers alongside the candle, too. And always remember—never leave burning candles unattended.

Tequila-Lime Shrimp

6 servings

2½ pounds unpeeled, large fresh
    shrimp
½ cup olive oil
¼ cup lime juice
¼ cup tequila
2 shallots, chopped
2 cloves garlic, minced
1 teaspoon salt
1 teaspoon ground cumin
½ teaspoon pepper

6 (12") metal skewers (see tip on
    page 110)

1 Peel shrimp, leaving tails intact; devein, if desired. Combine oil and remaining 7 ingredients in a bowl; stir in shrimp. Cover and chill 1 hour.

2 Remove shrimp from marinade, discarding marinade. Thread 9 shrimp onto each skewer. (Thread tail and neck of each shrimp onto skewers so shrimp will lie flat.)

3 Spray cold grill rack with nonstick cooking spray; preheat the grill over medium-high heat (350° to 400°). Place skewers on rack; grill, uncovered, about 3 to 4 minutes on each side or until shrimp turn pink.

Oven's an Option
This adults-only shrimp can be baked instead of grilled, if you'd rather. Just preheat the oven to 400°. Remove the shrimp from marinade, discarding marinade. Place the shrimp in an ungreased 10" x 15" rimmed baking sheet, and bake, uncovered, at 400° for 10 to 12 minutes or until the shrimp turn pink.

Fettuccine al Mascarpone

6 servings

1   (16-ounce) package dried fettuccine
2   tablespoons butter, softened

5   thin slices prosciutto, coarsely
    chopped (about 4 ounces)
¼   cup freshly grated Parmesan cheese
¾   teaspoon freshly ground pepper
½   teaspoon salt
4   ounces mascarpone cheese (see tip)

1 Cook pasta according to package directions; drain and toss with softened butter in a serving bowl.

2 Sprinkle prosciutto and next 3 ingredients over pasta; toss well. Add mascarpone, and toss pasta until well blended.

"Don't let the name of this dish scare you—it's just fancy mac and cheese! Mascarpone is a velvety-rich, creamy cheese with a delicate flavor. Readily available in the dairy section of the supermarket, mascarpone is the cheese of choice in tiramisù. It can be pricey, so if you need a substitute, try cream cheese."

Wild Mushroom and Fontina Pizza

4 servings

2   tablespoons olive oil
3   large shallots, thinly sliced
8   ounces shiitake mushrooms, stems
        removed (see tip)
3   large plum tomatoes, chopped
2   teaspoons dried thyme
2   tablespoons red wine vinegar
¼   teaspoon salt
¼   teaspoon pepper

1   (16-ounce) package prebaked Italian
        pizza bread shell
10   ounces fontina cheese, grated and
        divided
½   cup freshly grated Parmesan cheese

1 Heat olive oil in a large skillet over medium-high heat. Add shallots, and sauté 1 minute or until tender. Add mushrooms; cook 2 minutes, stirring constantly. Stir in tomatoes and next 4 ingredients; remove from heat.

2 Preheat the oven to 500°. Place bread shell on a 12" pizza pan. Top with three-quarters of the fontina cheese and all the vegetable mixture. Sprinkle with remaining cheeses. Bake at 500° for 12 minutes.

"Wild mushrooms and fontina cheese lend an exotic aura to this gourmet pizza. If you can't find shiitake mushrooms, substitute Portobello or crimini mushrooms. Both types have a rich, meaty flavor like shiitakes. Or use button mushrooms, which are mild in flavor and more widely available."

Presto Pesto Tart

4 main-dish or 8 appetizer servings

½   (15-ounce) package refrigerated pie
    crusts

2   cups (8 ounces) shredded
    mozzarella cheese, divided
5   plum tomatoes, sliced

½   cup mayonnaise
¼   cup grated Parmesan cheese
2   tablespoons prepared pesto
½   teaspoon freshly ground pepper

1 Preheat the oven to 425°. Unfold pie crust on a lightly greased baking sheet. Roll into a 12" circle. Brush outer 1" of crust with water. Fold edges up, and crimp. Prick bottom with a fork.

2 Bake at 425° for 8 to 10 minutes. Remove from oven. Sprinkle with 1 cup mozzarella cheese; let cool 15 minutes. Arrange tomato slices over cheese.

3 Stir together remaining 1 cup mozzarella cheese, the mayonnaise, and remaining 3 ingredients. Spread over tomato slices.

4 Reduce temperature to 375°, and bake at 375° for 20 minutes or until cheese melts and tart is thoroughly heated.

Make Mini Tarts!

Preheat the oven to 375°. Stir together ⅓ cup mayonnaise, ¼ cup shredded mozzarella cheese, 3 tablespoons grated Parmesan cheese, 2 teaspoons pesto, and ⅛ teaspoon pepper; stir in 2 chopped plum tomatoes. Spoon filling evenly into 1 (2.1-ounce) package miniature phyllo tart shells. Bake at 375° for 12 minutes. Yield: 15 tarts.

Easy Weeknight
Suppers

"Discover what 'hassle-free' really means when you cook up one of these suppertime favorites."

Slow-Cooker Fajitas

4 to 6 servings

1	medium onion, finely chopped
1	green bell pepper, thinly sliced
1	jalapeño pepper, seeded and finely chopped
2	cloves garlic, minced
2	teaspoons fajita seasoning, divided
1½	pounds lean flank steak, cut into 6 pieces
¾	teaspoon salt
1	(10-ounce) can diced tomatoes and green chilies, drained

6   (8") flour tortillas
Shredded Cheddar cheese
Sour cream

1 Layer first 4 ingredients in a 5-quart electric slow cooker. Sprinkle with 1 teaspoon fajita seasoning. Top with flank steak; sprinkle with salt and remaining 1 teaspoon fajita seasoning. Spoon drained tomatoes and green chilies over steak.

2 Cover and cook on HIGH setting 1 hour; reduce heat to LOW, and cook 6½ more hours.

3 Remove meat, and shred with a fork. Combine shredded meat with vegetable mixture in slow cooker.

4 Wrap tortillas in wax paper; microwave at HIGH 30 seconds. Spoon steak and vegetable mixture over warm tortillas; wrap or fold tortillas around mixture. Serve with cheese and sour cream.

"Wanna know my secret for keeping my fajitas together? Simply dab a bit of sour cream on the edges of the wrapped tortilla, and you have a nice little 'seal.'"

Easy Calzones

4 servings

¾ pound ground round
¼ cup chopped onion
3 cloves garlic, minced
1 (14-ounce) jar chunky spaghetti
    sauce, divided
½ teaspoon dried Italian seasoning

1 (11-ounce) can refrigerated French
    bread loaf
4 (1-ounce) mozzarella cheese slices
Nonstick cooking spray
Grated Parmesan cheese

1 Cook ground round, onion, and garlic in a large skillet over medium heat until ground round crumbles and is no longer pink; drain well. Return to skillet; stir in ½ cup spaghetti sauce and the Italian seasoning.

2 Preheat the oven to 400°. Unroll French bread loaf onto a lightly floured surface; roll or press with fingers into a 16" square. Cut into 4 squares; transfer dough squares to a lightly greased baking sheet. Spoon ground round mixture evenly into center of each square. Top each with a slice of mozzarella cheese. Fold over to form a triangle, pressing edges to seal. Coat triangles with cooking spray, and sprinkle with Parmesan cheese.

3 Bake at 400° for 12 to 15 minutes or until browned. Serve with remaining warmed spaghetti sauce.

MEALTIME MATTERS

Family Fun Night—Have a progressive dinner in your own home by serving each course in a different room. Remember to keep the menu simple. You want the dining diversion to be fun—not work!

No-Fuss Meatballs

(pictured on page 2)

3 dozen

1½   pounds ground beef
1   large egg, lightly beaten
¾   cup uncooked quick-cooking oats
¾   cup milk
1   teaspoon salt
1   teaspoon Italian seasoning
¼   teaspoon pepper

3   tablespoons all-purpose flour
1½   teaspoons paprika
½   teaspoon salt

1 Combine first 7 ingredients; shape into 1½" balls.

2 Preheat the oven to 400°. Combine flour, paprika, and ½ teaspoon salt. Gently roll meatballs in flour mixture, and place on a lightly greased rack in an aluminum foil-lined 9" x 13" pan.

3 Bake at 400° for 25 to 30 minutes. Drain on paper towels. Serve with your favorite sauce or with Weeknight Spaghetti on opposite page.

Meatball Magic

Make these meatballs ahead, and then freeze them for super-fast meatballs anytime. They're also great as appetizers and in sandwiches. To freeze, cool completely, and seal in an airtight container. To serve, place in a single layer on a baking sheet, and bake at 400° for 10 to 15 minutes.

Weeknight Spaghetti

(pictured on page 2)

6 to 8 servings

2 (28-ounce) cans diced tomatoes
1 (6-ounce) can tomato paste
1 cup water
1 teaspoon dried Italian seasoning
1½ teaspoons salt
¼ teaspoon black pepper
⅛ teaspoon ground red pepper

3 dozen frozen, cooked Italian-style
    meatballs, thawed
16 ounces spaghetti, cooked
Grated Parmesan cheese (optional)

1 Stir together first 7 ingredients in a large saucepan over medium-high heat. Reduce heat, and simmer 40 minutes, stirring occasionally.

2 Add meatballs; simmer 20 minutes. Serve over spaghetti, and sprinkle with grated Parmesan cheese, if desired.

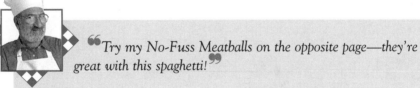

Try my No-Fuss Meatballs on the opposite page—they're great with this spaghetti!

Cheeseburger Macaroni

4 to 6 servings

8 ounces uncooked small elbow macaroni

1 pound ground beef
1 medium onion, chopped

2 (14½-ounce) cans Italian stewed tomatoes, undrained
¼ cup ketchup
1 teaspoon ground red pepper
½ teaspoon salt
1 cup (4 ounces) shredded Cheddar cheese

1 Cook elbow macaroni according to package directions; drain.

2 Cook ground beef and onion in a Dutch oven coated with nonstick cooking spray over medium-high heat until ground beef crumbles and is no longer pink. Drain well; pat with paper towels.

3 Stir stewed tomatoes and next 3 ingredients into skillet; cook until thoroughly heated. Stir in cooked macaroni. Sprinkle with shredded Cheddar cheese, and serve immediately.

"Got a cravin' for a beefy, cheesy dish? Then look no further! This robust entrée will quickly become a weeknight favorite at your house."

Six-Minute Pork Chops

6 to 8 servings

½   cup all-purpose flour
1   teaspoon salt
1   teaspoon seasoned pepper or
       black pepper
1½ pounds wafer-thin boneless pork
       chops

¼   cup vegetable oil

1 Combine first 3 ingredients in a shallow dish, and dredge pork chops in mixture.

2 Heat oil in a large skillet over medium-high heat. Add pork chops, and fry, in 3 batches, 1 minute on each side or until browned. Drain on paper towels.

"The key to this super-fast recipe is making sure your pork chops are wafer thin. That thinness ensures these chops are on the table in 6 minutes flat!"

Brunswick Stew-Cornbread Pie

6 to 8 servings

1   pound shredded barbecued pork
1   (16-ounce) package frozen
      vegetable gumbo mixture
1   (8½-ounce) can baby lima beans,
      drained
1   (8¼-ounce) can cream-style corn
1½ cups chicken broth
1   cup chopped cooked chicken
½   cup ketchup
½   cup barbecue sauce

1¾ cups self-rising cornmeal mix
1½ cups buttermilk
1   large egg, lightly beaten
2   tablespoons vegetable oil

1 Preheat the oven to 375°. Bring first 8 ingredients to a boil in a Dutch oven over medium heat; reduce heat, and simmer, uncovered, 15 minutes, stirring occasionally. Pour into a lightly greased 9" x 13" baking dish.

2 Stir together cornmeal mix and next 3 ingredients; spread evenly over stew mixture, leaving a ½" border.

3 Bake at 375° for 30 minutes or until cornbread is done.

"No, I didn't get out the smoker for this recipe. I picked up a pound of smoked meat, without the sauce, from my local barbecue joint—it's that easy! Or look for barbecue meat in the freezer section of your supermarket. It's a winner either way!"

Lucky Black-Eyed Peas and Ham

4 servings

2 tablespoons vegetable oil
1 medium onion, chopped

2 (15-ounce) cans black-eyed peas, rinsed and drained
¾ cup chopped cooked ham
¼ cup teriyaki sauce
½ teaspoon Creole seasoning
1¼ cups water
Warm cooked rice

1 Heat oil in a medium saucepan over medium-high 3 minutes. Add chopped onion, and sauté 3 minutes.

2 Add peas and next 4 ingredients. Bring to a boil; reduce heat, and simmer 15 minutes, stirring occasionally. Serve over warm cooked rice. Top with chopped tomatoes and sliced green onions, if desired.

MEALTIME MATTERS

New Year's Tradition—You'll be dishing out luck around the table when you serve your gang these black-eyed peas. Plan a special New Year's Day celebration with this recipe as the main dish. Don't forget to add some type of "greens" to bring financial rewards. Afterward, have everyone toss their New Year's resolutions and predictions into a basket; then draw at random, and guess who said what.

Hot Ham-and-Cheese Roll-Ups

4 servings

1   (10-ounce) can refrigerated pizza
     crust
2   tablespoons chopped fresh basil or
     2 teaspoons dried basil
6   ounces thinly sliced maple-glazed
     ham
1   cup (4 ounces) shredded mozzarella
     cheese

1 Preheat the oven to 400°. Roll out dough to a 12" square. Sprinkle with basil to ½" from edges. Top with ham slices, and sprinkle with cheese to ½" from edges.

2 Roll up dough, beginning at 1 end; place seam side down on an aluminum foil-lined baking sheet coated with nonstick cooking spray.

3 Bake at 400° for 20 to 25 minutes or until golden brown. Cool 5 minutes. Cut into 1½" slices. Serve roll-ups with pasta sauce or mustard, if desired.

Lunchtime Ease
These roll-ups easily reheat in the microwave. Just cook on HIGH 1 minute or until thoroughly heated— it makes a perfect lunch for an active family.

Grilled Bratwurst Sandwiches

6 servings

6   bratwurst links (about 1½ pounds)

2   tablespoons butter
2   large onions, thinly sliced
1   medium-size green bell pepper, cut
    into thin strips
1   medium-size red bell pepper, cut
    into thin strips

2   (12-ounce) bottles beer (do not use
    dark)
2   teaspoons salt-free seasoning blend

6   hoagie rolls, split

1 Preheat the grill. Grill bratwurst, covered, over medium-high heat (350° to 400°) for 10 to 15 minutes or until thoroughly heated, turning once.

2 Melt butter in a large skillet over medium heat; add onions and bell pepper strips, and cook until tender.

3 Stir in beer and seasoning blend; add sausage, and simmer mixture for 20 minutes.

4 Place 1 bratwurst link in each roll, and top evenly with vegetable mixture. Serve with your favorite mustard, if desired.

MEALTIME MATTERS

Good "News"!—For a no-fuss table cover when eating outdoors, line your table with newspaper. When dinner's over, just roll up the newspaper and your cleanup is done! Then you can get on to more fun activities.

Corn Dogs and 'Taters

8 servings

16 (8") rounded wooden sticks
8   frankfurters
2   baking potatoes, cut into ½" cubes
    (about ¾ pound)

¾   cup all-purpose flour
½   teaspoon baking powder
½   teaspoon salt
1   large egg
½   cup milk
1   tablespoon vegetable oil

Peanut oil

1 Insert a stick into each frankfurter, leaving about a 3" handle; set aside. Thread potatoes onto remaining sticks.

2 Whisk together flour and next 5 ingredients; pour into a tall glass.

3 Pour peanut oil into a large skillet to a depth of 1½"; heat to 350°.

4 Dip frankfurters in batter, covering well. Fry frankfurters and potatoes, in batches, 4 to 5 minutes or until golden brown. Serve with mustard and ketchup, if desired.

Make 'em Snappy!

If you're crunched for time, substitute an 8-ounce package of hush puppy mix and ¾ cup milk or an 8½ ounce package corn muffin mix, 1 egg, and ⅓ cup milk for the batter mixture. Whatever your choice, you'll have a surefire winner for your gang!

Cheesy Chilie Chicken

4 servings

1   teaspoon ground black pepper
¼   teaspoon ground red pepper
½   teaspoon paprika
½   teaspoon garlic powder
4   skinned and boned chicken breast
     halves

1   tablespoon butter
1   (4.5-ounce) can diced green chilies
1   cup (4 ounces) shredded Monterey
     Jack cheese

1 Combine first 4 ingredients; sprinkle evenly over chicken.

2 Melt butter in a large skillet over medium-high heat. Add chicken, and cook 2 to 3 minutes on each side or until golden brown. Remove from heat; top evenly with chilies and cheese. Cover and let stand 2 to 3 minutes or until cheese melts. Sprinkle with additional paprika, if desired.

"Moms, your family will love my cheesy chicken, and you will, too. It can be on the table in less than 30 minutes from start to finish...no kidding! It's great served with Mexican rice. Look for those easy-to-prepare packets in your grocery store."

Crispy Onion Baked Chicken

4 servings

1   cup fine, dry breadcrumbs
    (prepared)
1   (1.4-ounce) package dry onion
    soup mix

4   skinned and boned chicken breast
    halves
⅓   cup mayonnaise

1 Preheat the oven to 425°. Combine breadcrumbs and soup mix in a large zip-top plastic bag; seal and shake well.

2 Brush chicken breasts with mayonnaise; place chicken breasts, 1 at a time, in bag. Seal and shake to coat. Arrange chicken on an ungreased rack in a broiler pan. Bake at 425° for 20 to 25 minutes or until done.

"The French onion soup mix adds crunch and crispness to my chicken while the mayonnaise contributes to its moistness. And by baking in a broiler pan, the chicken will keep its crispy coating."

Skillet Chicken 'n' Noodles

4 servings

2   teaspoons vegetable oil
1   pound skinned and boned chicken
      breast halves, cut into ¼" strips
      (about 3 chicken breast halves)

2   cups fresh broccoli florets
1¾ cups water
1   (4½-ounce) jar mushrooms, drained
3   tablespoons soy sauce
2   (3-ounce) packages ramen chicken
      noodle soup mix

1 Heat oil in a large nonstick skillet over medium-high heat until hot. Add chicken strips, and cook 5 minutes or until done, stirring often.

2 Add broccoli and next 3 ingredients. Stir in 1 flavor packet from soup mix. (Reserve remaining flavor packet for another use.) Bring broccoli mixture to a boil. Break noodles from both packages of soup mix in half, and add to skillet. Cover, reduce heat, and simmer 5 to 7 minutes or until broccoli and noodles are tender, stirring occasionally.

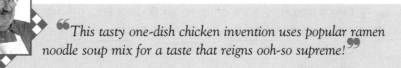

"This tasty one-dish chicken invention uses popular ramen noodle soup mix for a taste that reigns ooh-so supreme!"

Quick Chicken 'n' Dumplings

4 to 6 servings

4   cups water

3   cups chopped cooked chicken
     (see tip)

2   (10¾-ounce) cans cream of chicken
     soup, undiluted

2   teaspoons chicken bouillon granules

1   teaspoon seasoned pepper or black
     pepper

1   (7.5-ounce) can refrigerated
     buttermilk biscuits

1 Bring first 5 ingredients to a boil in a Dutch oven over medium-high heat, stirring often.

2 Separate each biscuit in half, forming 2 rounds; cut each round in half. Drop biscuit pieces, 1 at a time, into boiling mixture; stir gently. Cover, reduce heat to low, and simmer, stirring occasionally, 15 to 20 minutes.

Chicken Choices
One roasted whole chicken or 6 skinned and boned cooked chicken breast halves yield about 3 cups of chopped meat. You can cook your own or find chopped cooked chicken in the freezer section at your supermarket.

Speedy Chicken Enchiladas

8 servings

2 tablespoons vegetable oil
1 medium onion, chopped
1 (19-ounce) can enchilada sauce
1 (16-ounce) can black beans, rinsed
   and drained
1 (14½-ounce) can diced tomatoes
   with jalapeños
1 (11-ounce) can Mexican-style corn,
   drained
1 teaspoon fajita seasoning or chili
   powder

1 (10-ounce) package 6" corn tortillas
3 cups chopped cooked chicken
3 cups (12 ounces) shredded Mexican
   four-cheese blend

1 Heat vegetable oil in a large skillet over medium-high heat. Add onion, and sauté until tender. Stir in enchilada sauce and next 4 ingredients. Reduce heat to low, and cook 5 minutes or until thoroughly heated, stirring often.

2 Preheat the oven to 350°. Spoon ⅓ sauce mixture into a lightly greased 9" x 13" baking dish. Layer with ⅓ tortillas, half of chicken, and 1 cup cheese. Repeat layers with ⅓ each of sauce mixture and tortillas, remaining chicken, and 1 cup cheese. Top with remaining tortillas, sauce mixture, and cheese.

3 Bake at 350° for 15 to 20 minutes or until golden and bubbly.

Beef It Up!
Vary this Tex-Mex casserole by substituting ground beef for chicken. Just use 2 pounds of cooked, lean ground beef.

Chicken-and-Sausage Jambalaya

6 to 8 servings

1   (16-ounce) package Cajun-style smoked sausage, cut into ¼" slices
2   celery ribs, chopped
1   medium onion, chopped
1   medium-size green bell pepper, chopped

4   cups chopped cooked chicken
1   (32-ounce) container chicken broth
1½ cups uncooked long-grain rice
1   tablespoon Cajun seasoning

1 Cook smoked sausage in a Dutch oven over medium heat, stirring constantly, 3 minutes or until browned. Add celery, onion, and bell pepper, and sauté 6 to 8 minutes or until vegetables are tender.

2 Stir in chicken and remaining ingredients; bring to a boil. Cover, reduce heat, and simmer 45 minutes or until rice is done and liquid is absorbed. Remove from heat, and let stand 10 to 15 minutes before serving.

MEALTIME MATTERS

One-Dish Ease—Take the edge off the dinnertime rush with this doable weeknight recipe. Because this dish is prepared in one pot, you'll have less to clean up, giving you more family time. All you need to complete your meal is a salad and some crusty French bread.

Mama's Chicken Pot Pie

(pictured on cover)

6 servings

1   (10¾-ounce) can cream of celery or
     cream of chicken soup, undiluted
1½   cups chicken broth

3   cups chopped cooked chicken
1   (10-ounce) package frozen mixed
     vegetables
¼   teaspoon salt
¼   teaspoon pepper

½   cup butter
1   cup self-rising flour
¾   cup milk

1 Preheat the oven to 400°. Cook soup in a medium saucepan over medium heat until hot. Gradually add broth, stirring until smooth.

2 Add chicken, frozen vegetables, salt, and pepper. Bring to a boil; reduce heat, and simmer, uncovered, 10 minutes, stirring occasionally. Spoon mixture into a lightly greased 7" x 11" baking dish; set aside.

3 Cut butter into flour with a pastry blender or 2 knives until mixture is crumbly. Add milk, stirring just until dry ingredients are moistened. (Mixture will be lumpy.)

4 Gently spoon batter evenly on top of chicken mixture. Bake, uncovered, at 400° for 35 minutes or until golden.

M-m-m…the aroma of this chicken pot pie baking in the oven takes me back to the warmth of Mama's cozy kitchen—but without all the fuss and mess! My version uses frozen vegetables with an easy homemade crust. Make this family favorite tonight, and you'll have 'em beggin' for it again and again!

Soft Taco Stacks

(pictured on page 38)

4 to 6 servings

1   (16-ounce) can refried beans
9   (10") flour tortillas, divided
1   (8-ounce) package shredded
        Mexican four-cheese blend
2   jalapeño peppers, seeded and
        chopped
1½ cups chopped cooked chicken

1½ cups shredded lettuce
1   (8-ounce) jar salsa
1   medium avocado, diced
2   medium tomatoes, seeded and
        chopped
⅓   cup chopped fresh cilantro

1 Preheat the oven to 350°. Spread beans on 1 side each of 3 tortillas; place tortillas, beans side up, on a baking sheet. Sprinkle evenly with cheese and next 2 ingredients.

2 Bake at 350° for 10 minutes or until cheese melts. Remove from baking sheet.

3 Sprinkle 3 baked tortillas evenly with lettuce; top each with 1 tortilla. Spread each tortilla top with 2 table-spoons salsa, and sprinkle evenly with avocado, tomatoes, and cilantro; top with remaining 3 tortillas. Cut into quarters; serve with remaining salsa.

Lighten Up!
Make this recipe figure-friendly by using fat-free refried beans and 2% reduced-fat cheese. You'll still get that same great taste with less fat and calories!

Fried Catfish Sandwiches

(pictured on page 39)

4 servings

¾ cup yellow cornmeal
¼ cup all-purpose flour
1½ teaspoons salt
1 teaspoon ground red pepper
¼ teaspoon garlic powder
4 catfish fillets (about 1½ pounds)

Vegetable oil

4 onion sandwich buns, split and toasted
Cocktail or tartar sauce
Lettuce leaves
4 tomato slices (optional)

1 Combine first 5 ingredients in a large shallow dish. Dredge fish in mixture, coating well.

2 Pour oil into a Dutch oven to a depth of 3"; heat to 370° to 375°. Fry fish 4 to 5 minutes on each side or until golden brown. Drain on paper towels.

3 Serve on sandwich buns with cocktail sauce, lettuce, and, if desired, tomato slices.

"A good indicator to determine if the oil is hot enough is to sprinkle some cornmeal in the pan. If it sizzles immediately, you're ready to fry!"

81

Quick Fish Fillets

2 servings

1	pound orange roughy fillets

¼   cup fine, dry breadcrumbs
       (prepared)
1   teaspoon chopped fresh parsley
½   teaspoon paprika

¼   cup plain yogurt
1   teaspoon prepared mustard

1 Preheat the oven to 450°. Cut orange roughy into serving-size pieces.

2 Combine breadcrumbs, parsley, and paprika in a shallow dish.

3 Combine yogurt and mustard. Dip fillets in yogurt mixture, and dredge in breadcrumb mixture; place on a baking sheet coated with nonstick cooking spray.

4 Bake at 450° for 20 minutes. Serve with lemon wedges, if desired.

Zap It!
This recipe results in fantastic fish from the microwave, too! Prepare as directed in Steps 2 and 3, and microwave at HIGH, covered with a paper towel, 4 minutes or until fish flakes easily with a fork.

Tuna Melts

4 servings

1   (12-ounce) can white tuna in water, drained
2   celery ribs, chopped
3   tablespoons mayonnaise
2   tablespoons Dijon mustard
2   teaspoons lime juice
½   teaspoon pepper
4   English muffins, split
8   tomato slices
8   (1-ounce) Swiss cheese slices

1 Preheat the oven to Broil. Stir together first 6 ingredients; spread evenly on each English muffin half. Top each muffin half with 1 tomato slice and 1 cheese slice.

2 Broil sandwiches 5½" from heat 5 minutes or until cheese melts.

MEALTIME MATTERS

Sandwich Night—Start a weekly routine at your house with sandwich night. It's a great idea for a no-hassle meal! For variety, serve sandwiches on different types of bread and with different toppings. Add chips, corn on the cob, or fresh fruit for a simple side to a casual dinner.

Busy-Night Breakfast Bake

6 servings

1   pound hot or mild ground pork
       sausage
½   (16-ounce) package frozen
       shredded hash brown potatoes
       (about 3 cups)
1   cup (4 ounces) shredded sharp
       Cheddar cheese

6   large eggs, beaten
¾   cup milk
¾   teaspoon dry mustard
½   teaspoon salt
Dash of pepper

1 Brown sausage in a large skillet, stirring until it crumbles and is no longer pink; drain. Layer potatoes, sausage, and cheese in a greased 9" x 13" baking dish.

2 Combine eggs and next 4 ingredients; pour over sausage mixture. Cover and chill 8 hours.

3 Preheat the oven to 350°. Bake, covered, at 350° for 30 minutes; uncover and bake 5 more minutes or until set. Let stand 10 minutes before serving.

MEALTIME ✕ MATTERS

Breakfast for Supper—Breakfast is good any time of day, so why not serve it for supper? It'll be a fun change for your family. Plus this is a great make-ahead recipe—perfect for those hectic evenings. Just stick it in the oven and breakfast's—I mean supper's—on!

Cheesy Pasta Bake

8 servings

2 tablespoons butter
¼ cup all-purpose flour
3 cups milk

4 cups (16 ounces) shredded extra-
  sharp Cheddar cheese
¾ cup shredded Parmesan cheese,
  divided
¾ teaspoon salt
1 teaspoon freshly ground black
  pepper
½ teaspoon ground red pepper
16 ounces rotini or penne pasta,
  cooked

1 Preheat the oven to 350°. Melt butter in a Dutch oven over medium heat; whisk in flour until smooth. Gradually whisk in milk, and cook 3 minutes or until thickened, whisking constantly.

2 Add Cheddar cheese, ¼ cup Parmesan cheese, the salt, black pepper, and red pepper, whisking until cheese melts. Add pasta, tossing to coat.

3 Pour mixture into a lightly greased 9" x 13" baking dish. Sprinkle with remaining ½ cup Parmesan cheese. Bake at 350° for 5 minutes or until cheese melts.

MEALTIME ✕ MATTERS

No-Fuss Flowers—For a quick centerpiece, line a basket with plastic wrap. Place container plants, such as gerbera daisies, marigolds, or African violets, in the basket. Fill in around the plants with Spanish moss. Voilà! In a week or so, plant the flowers outdoors.

Plum Tomato Pizza Squares

6 servings

1 (10-ounce) can refrigerated pizza crust

1½ cups (6 ounces) shredded pizza cheese blend, divided
⅔ cup mayonnaise
2 tablespoons chopped fresh basil
2 teaspoons prepared minced garlic
⅛ teaspoon salt
¼ teaspoon Italian seasoning
4 plum tomatoes, thinly sliced

1 Preheat the oven to 350°. Fit pizza crust onto a lightly greased 10" x 15" rimmed baking sheet. Bake at 350° for 10 minutes or until lightly browned.

2 Increase the oven temperature to 375°. Stir together 1 cup cheese, the mayonnaise, and next 4 ingredients; spread mixture over pizza crust. Top with sliced tomatoes, and sprinkle with remaining ½ cup cheese.

3 Bake at 375° for 15 minutes. Cut into squares to serve.

MEALTIME ✕ MATTERS

Dinnertime Traditions—Make Friday night pizza night. Or how 'bout making Sunday soup night? Whatever the dish, identify a special mealtime for a certain day of the week—or even month. It'll give the family a new tradition to look forward to and to even help plan!

Simple Red Beans and Rice

8 servings

1 tablespoon vegetable oil
1 pound smoked sausage, thinly
   sliced
1 medium onion, chopped
1 medium-size green bell pepper,
   chopped
1 clove garlic, minced
3 (15-ounce) cans red beans, rinsed
   and drained
1 (16-ounce) can tomato paste
1 (14½-ounce) can stewed tomatoes,
   undrained and chopped
1½ cups water
¼ teaspoon dried oregano
¼ teaspoon hot sauce
1 bay leaf

Warm cooked rice

1 Heat vegetable oil in a Dutch oven over medium-high heat. Add sausage and next 3 ingredients, and sauté 8 minutes or until vegetables are tender. Add beans and next 6 ingredients.

2 Bring to a boil; cover, reduce heat, and simmer 20 minutes. **Remove and discard bay leaf.** Serve over rice.

"Leftovers are even better the next day—especially because you don't have to start from scratch! To reheat this one-dish meal, microwave at MEDIUM (50% power) 3 to 5 minutes or until thoroughly heated."

Corn Waffles with Cilantro-Lime Butter

10 (4") waffles

1¾ cups self-rising flour
⅓ cup sugar
½ teaspoon salt

3 large eggs
½ cup buttermilk
⅓ cup vegetable oil
1 cup frozen whole kernel corn,
 thawed

Cilantro-Lime Butter (see recipe below)

1 Combine first 3 ingredients in a large bowl, and make a well in center of mixture.

2 Whisk together eggs, buttermilk, and vegetable oil; stir in corn. Pour into well of flour mixture, stirring just until moistened.

3 Cook in a preheated, oiled waffle iron until golden. Serve with Cilantro-Lime Butter, honey, or maple syrup.

Cilantro-Lime Butter

½ cup butter, softened
1 tablespoon chopped fresh cilantro
1 teaspoon grated lime
1 teaspoon fresh lime juice

1 Stir together all ingredients until well blended. Yield: ½ cup.

Feisty Flavor
Fresh cilantro has a distinctive taste, and one thing's for sure—people either love it or loathe it! For taste, it's unequaled. So we don't suggest a substitute.

Super Sideshow

66Accent your meal
with one of these
tempting sides.
They're a snap to
make, and ooh-so-
good to eat!99

Golden Apples

4 servings

1 Granny Smith apple, cored and cut
   into ¼"-thick slices
2 Rome apples, cored and cut into
   ¼"-thick slices
½ cup orange juice

¼ cup honey
2 tablespoons apricot preserves

1 Combine apple slices and orange
  juice in a large skillet; bring to a boil
over high heat.

2 Stir honey and apricot preserves into
  apple mixture; reduce heat, and simmer, uncovered, 4 to 5 minutes or until
apples are tender. Serve warm.

"Try my little secret to make your cleanup easier. Before pouring the honey into the measuring cup, spray the cup with nonstick cooking spray. The honey will slide right out."

Couscous Amandine

8 to 10 servings

2   cups water
1   (10-ounce) package couscous
½   cup raisins
½   teaspoon salt

½   cup slivered almonds, toasted
¼   cup chopped fresh parsley
2   tablespoons olive oil
½   teaspoon ground cinnamon

1 Bring water to a boil in a medium saucepan; stir in couscous, raisins, and salt. Cover, remove from heat, and let stand 5 minutes. Fluff couscous mixture with a fork.

2 Stir in almonds and remaining ingredients. Serve immediately.

Flavor Boost

Toasting brings out the maximum flavor in any kind of nut. To toast almonds, place in a small skillet, and cook over medium heat 5 to 7 minutes or until lightly browned, stirring often.

Pasta Alfredo

4 side-dish or 2 main-dish servings

1 tablespoon olive oil
⅓ cup diced cooked ham
1 large red bell pepper, diced
1 clove garlic, minced
1 (10-ounce) container fresh Alfredo
   sauce
1 teaspoon dried sage
½ teaspoon freshly ground black
   pepper

2 cups bow tie pasta, uncooked
¼ cup freshly grated Parmesan cheese

1 Heat olive oil in a large skillet over medium-high heat. Add ham, red bell pepper, and garlic; cook 3 minutes, stirring often. Reduce heat to medium-low; stir in Alfredo sauce, sage, and black pepper. Cook until thoroughly heated, stirring constantly.

2 Meanwhile, cook pasta according to package directions; drain. Add pasta to skillet; toss well. Sprinkle with cheese.

"The secret to getting this dish on the table quickly is the prepared Alfredo sauce. And if it's just the two of you, consider serving it with a salad and bread for a get-it-on-the-table-fast meal."

Lemon Rice Pilaf

6 servings

2 tablespoons butter
4 celery ribs, sliced
6 green onions, chopped

3 cups warm cooked rice
2 tablespoons grated lemon rind
½ teaspoon salt
¼ teaspoon pepper

1 Melt butter in a large skillet over medium-high heat; add celery and green onions, and sauté until celery is tender.

2 Stir in rice and remaining ingredients; cook over low heat 2 minutes or until thoroughly heated.

MEALTIME MATTERS

Guest of Honor—Pick a night for your child to play host to a special dinner guest. And be sure to include your child in the meal planning—and serving—as well as any extras that will make his or her guest feel welcome.

Easy Baked Risotto

4 servings

1	tablespoon butter
1	small onion, minced
¾	cup uncooked Arborio rice (see tip)
1	(14½-ounce) can chicken broth
½	teaspoon dried Italian seasoning
¼	teaspoon salt
¼	teaspoon pepper

1 Preheat the oven to 350°. Melt butter in a 10" ovenproof skillet over medium heat; add onion, and sauté until tender. Add rice; cook 3 minutes, stirring constantly. Stir in broth, and bring to a boil. Stir in Italian seasoning and remaining ingredients.

2 Bake, covered, at 350° for 30 minutes or until liquid is absorbed.

The Right Rice

Arborio rice is the rice of choice when making risotto. This Italian-grown rice is shorter and plumper than most short-grain rice, and because of its high starch content, it yields risotto's creamy texture when cooked. Arborio rice is sold in most supermarkets, but you can also substitute long- or whole-grain rice for Arborio.

Roasted Asparagus with Thyme

4 servings

1½ pounds fresh asparagus
1   large clove garlic, halved

2   teaspoons olive oil
½   teaspoon salt
¼   teaspoon freshly ground pepper
¼   teaspoon dried thyme

1 Preheat the oven to 400°. Snap off tough ends of asparagus. Rub cut sides of garlic over bottom and sides of an ungreased 9" x 13" baking dish.

2 Place asparagus and garlic in dish. Drizzle with olive oil. Sprinkle with salt, pepper, and thyme; toss gently. Bake, uncovered, at 400° for 20 minutes, stirring once.

Roasted Goodness

Roasting veggies enhances their natural sweetness, and it's a cinch to do. Cut similarly textured veggies the same size, and place on a rimmed baking sheet in a single layer. Don't overcrowd your pan. Drizzle the veggies with olive oil, sprinkle with salt and pepper, and roast. As a general rule, roast delicate veggies such as asparagus at 400°. Turn up the heat between 450° and 500° to roast sturdy root veggies such as potatoes. Roasted veggies pair deliciously with most entrées and casseroles.

Black Beans 'n' Rice

3 servings

1   (4.6-ounce) package boil-in-bag
       long-grain rice

1   (15.5-ounce) can black beans,
       undrained

1   tablespoon extra-spicy salt-free herb
       blend

⅛   teaspoon pepper

½   cup (2 ounces) shredded sharp
       Cheddar cheese

⅓   cup finely chopped onion

1   medium tomato, chopped

1 Cook rice according to package
directions.

2 Combine beans, herb blend, and
pepper in a large saucepan; bring
to a boil over medium heat, stirring
constantly.

3 Spoon rice onto a serving platter.
Pour bean mixture over rice. Top
with cheese, onion, and tomato.

"These cheesy beans can be a side dish or main dish. I like to have cornbread on the side when I serve it as a main-dish meal."

Green Beans with Garlic-Herb Butter

4 servings

1	pound fresh green beans, trimmed
¼	cup butter
1	small onion, minced
1	celery rib, minced
1½	teaspoons prepared minced garlic
¼	teaspoon chopped fresh or dried rosemary
¾	teaspoon salt
¼	cup chopped fresh parsley or 1 tablespoon dried parsley

1 Cover beans with water in a large saucepan. Bring to a boil, and boil 10 minutes or until crisp-tender. Drain. Plunge beans into ice water to stop the cooking process; drain again.

2 Melt butter in a large saucepan over medium-high heat; add onion and celery, and sauté 5 minutes. Add garlic, and sauté 2 minutes. Stir in beans, rosemary, salt, and parsley; sauté 4 minutes or until thoroughly heated.

"A savory garlic and herb butter pumps up the flavor of these garden-fresh beans. Serve alongside your favorite entrée tonight!"

Broccoli-Rice Casserole

6 servings

2   (10-ounce) packages frozen broccoli
    florets

2   cups cooked rice
1   (10¾-ounce) can cream of
    mushroom soup, undiluted
½   (15-ounce) jar process cheese
    spread

3   tablespoons saltine cracker crumbs

1 Place broccoli in a 2-quart microwave-safe baking dish. Cover and microwave at HIGH 8 to 10 minutes or until crisp-tender; drain.

2 Meanwhile, stir together rice, soup, and cheese spread in a large bowl. Stir in broccoli.

3 Wipe baking dish dry, and coat with nonstick cooking spray. Pour mixture into baking dish; sprinkle with cracker crumbs. Microwave, uncovered, at HIGH 8 to 10 minutes or until casserole is thoroughly heated.

MEALTIME MATTERS

Group Effort—Involve the whole gang in the meal before you sit down to eat. Have someone set the table, pour the drinks, or stir up the ingredients for this family-pleasin' casserole.

Sweet 'n' Tangy Carrots

4 servings

1   pound carrots, peeled and sliced
        diagonally, or 1 (16-ounce)
        package frozen sliced carrots
¼   cup orange juice
1   tablespoon lime juice
2   teaspoons butter
½   teaspoon salt

⅓   cup honey
1   teaspoon minced fresh ginger
        (optional)
½   teaspoon grated orange rind
½   teaspoon grated lime rind

1 Cook first 5 ingredients in a 2-quart saucepan over medium heat 20 minutes or until carrots are tender, stirring often.

2 Remove from heat; stir in honey and remaining ingredients.

"Get double-duty from your orange and lime by grating the rind before squeezing for the juice."

Glazed Carrots and Parsnips

6 servings

½ pound carrots, peeled (about 4)
½ pound parsnips, peeled (about 6)

2 tablespoons dried currants (optional)

2 tablespoons butter
2 tablespoons whole-grain mustard
2 tablespoons honey
¼ teaspoon salt
1 tablespoon chopped fresh parsley

1 Cut carrots and parsnips into ¼" x 2" strips.

2 Cover carrots and parsnips with water in a large saucepan. Bring to a boil, and boil 10 to 12 minutes or until tender, adding currants, if desired, during the last 2 minutes; drain.

3 Melt butter in large saucepan over medium heat; stir in mustard, honey, and salt until blended. Stir in carrot mixture, and cook until thoroughly heated. Sprinkle with chopped parsley.

Carrot Pointers

Carrots are available year-round and are a great source of vitamin A. Look for firm, smooth carrots with a deep orange color—avoid those with cracks. Generally, 1 pound of carrots equals about 3 cups chopped or sliced, or about 2½ cups shredded.

Cauliflower-Broccoli Fritters

6 to 8 servings

½   pound fresh broccoli florets
½   pound fresh cauliflower florets
2   cups boiling water

2   large eggs, lightly beaten
1   small onion, diced
½   cup chopped pecans, toasted
½   cup self-rising flour
½   teaspoon salt

Vegetable oil

1 Cook florets in 2 cups boiling water in a Dutch oven over medium heat 10 to 12 minutes or until very tender; drain.

2 Mash florets with a fork or potato masher in a large bowl. Stir in eggs and next 4 ingredients.

3 Pour oil into a large skillet to a depth of ¼"; heat to 350°. Drop vegetable mixture by tablespoonfuls into hot oil; cook, in batches, 1 to 2 minutes on each side or until lightly browned. Drain on paper towels, and keep warm.

"You won't have to bribe your kids to eat their broccoli or cauliflower once they pop these crispy fried treats in their mouths! They'll be beggin' for more!"

Creamed Corn

8 servings

4   (10-ounce) packages frozen whole
      kernel corn, thawed
2   cups whipping cream
2   tablespoons sugar
1   teaspoon salt
⅛   teaspoon ground red pepper

2   tablespoons butter
2   tablespoons all-purpose flour
¾   cup freshly grated Parmesan
      cheese, divided

1 Preheat the oven to Broil. Combine first 5 ingredients in a large saucepan. Bring to a boil over medium heat, stirring occasionally. Reduce heat, and simmer, uncovered, 5 minutes.

2 Meanwhile, microwave butter in a microwave-safe dish at HIGH 45 to 50 seconds or until melted. Add flour, stirring until smooth. Stir into corn mixture; remove from heat. Stir in ½ cup cheese. Pour mixture into an ungreased 7" x 11" baking dish; sprinkle with remaining ¼ cup cheese. Broil 5½" from heat 4 to 5 minutes or until cheese melts.

"Freshly grated Parmesan cheese and ground red pepper zap this creamed corn recipe with unexpected flair."

102

Bacon Mashed Potatoes

7 servings

1   (22-ounce) package frozen mashed
     potatoes

1   (8-ounce) package finely shredded
     colby-Monterey Jack cheese
7   bacon slices, cooked and crumbled
4   green onions, chopped
2   cloves garlic, minced
½   cup sour cream
¼   cup butter, softened
¾   teaspoon salt
½   teaspoon pepper

1 Prepare mashed potatoes according
to package directions.

2 Stir in cheese and remaining ingredients. Serve immediately.

Lighten Up

These super-easy mashed potatoes can easily be lightened. Substitute shredded light Mexican cheese blend, reduced-fat bacon, and nonfat sour cream for the regular products. You can even cut the amount of butter in half if you want to!

Down-Home Succotash

(pictured on facing page)

6 to 8 servings

1 (10-ounce) package frozen petite
    lima beans

1 (16-ounce) package frozen yellow
    and white corn, thawed

2 tablespoons butter
2 tablespoons all-purpose flour
1 teaspoon sugar
½ teaspoon salt
½ teaspoon seasoned pepper or black
    pepper
1¼ cups milk

1 Cook lima beans according to pack-age directions; drain.

2 Pulse corn in a food processor 8 to 10 times or until coarsely chopped.

3 Melt butter in large saucepan over medium heat; add flour, stirring until smooth. Cook 1 minute, stirring con-stantly; stir in sugar, salt, and pepper. Gradually add milk, stirring until smooth.

4 Stir in corn, and cook 12 to 15 min-utes or until corn is tender and mixture is thickened, stirring often. Stir in drained lima beans. Garnish with cooked, crumbled bacon, if desired, and serve immediately.

"Make the most of frozen foods and the staples you keep in your pantry to whip up this favorite classic tonight."

Mexi Stew in a Biscuit Bowl,
page 122

Mama's Mini-Cinnis,
page 139

Honey-Baked Tomatoes

(pictured on facing page)

8 servings

8   medium-size ripe tomatoes, cut into
       1" slices
4   teaspoons honey

2   white bread slices
1   tablespoon dried tarragon
1½ teaspoons salt
2   teaspoons freshly ground pepper
4   teaspoons butter

1 Preheat the oven to 350°. Place tomato slices in a single layer in a lightly greased 9" x 13" baking dish. Drizzle with honey, spreading honey into hollows of tomato slices.

2 Process bread in a food processor or blender until finely crumbled. Stir together breadcrumbs, tarragon, and next 2 ingredients; sprinkle evenly over tomato slices. Dot with butter.

3 Bake at 350° for 30 minutes or until tomato skins begin to wrinkle. Increase oven temperature to Broil. Broil 5½" from heat 5 minutes or until tops are golden. Serve warm.

"This is a good recipe to prepare for company. For one thing, tomatoes go with anything! And second, we can get a jump on the preparation. The crumb topping can be made a day ahead. Then we can prepare and bake the tomatoes about an hour before serving time and just keep them warm in a 200° oven."

Easy Veggie Kabobs

4 servings

8   small mushroom caps
2   small zucchini, cut into 8 slices
1   medium-size yellow bell pepper, cut into ½" to ¾" pieces
1   small red onion, cut into 1½" pieces
4   (12") metal skewers

½   cup butter, melted
1   tablespoon chopped fresh basil
1   teaspoon garlic powder

1 Thread vegetables evenly onto skewers. (See tip.)

2 Stir together melted butter, basil, and garlic powder; reserve ¼ cup butter mixture, and set aside.

3 Spray cold grill rack with nonstick cooking spray; preheat the grill to medium-high heat. Place vegetable skewers on rack; grill, covered, 20 to 25 minutes or until vegetables are tender, turning and basting with remaining butter mixture every 5 minutes. Serve with reserved ¼ cup butter mixture.

Skewer Tips

If you use wooden skewers, be sure to soak 'em in water for 30 minutes so they won't burn as the food cooks. You'll also need to leave a little space between each chunk of food as you're threading it onto the skewer to ensure even cooking.

Nutty Yams

4 servings

1   (29-ounce) can yams, drained
⅓   cup chopped macadamia nuts
⅓   cup packed brown sugar
⅓   cup flaked coconut
3   tablespoons all-purpose flour
3   tablespoons butter, melted

1 Preheat the oven to 350°. Place yams in an ungreased 1-quart baking dish. Combine nuts and remaining 4 ingredients, stirring until mixture is crumbly. Sprinkle nut mixture over yams. Bake, uncovered, at 350° for 35 minutes.

MEALTIME ✕ MATTERS

Thanksgiving Blessings—When your family gathers for the annual feast, pass a "blessings book" around the table for each person to record a special memory. Later you can add photos of the day. Add to it each year or have relatives add to it each year so you can enjoy reading everyone's thoughts from previous years.

Parmesan-Zucchini Sticks

6 servings

½ cup fine, dry breadcrumbs
    (prepared)
½ cup grated Parmesan cheese
3 medium zucchini
1 large egg, lightly beaten

Vegetable oil
½ teaspoon salt

1 Combine breadcrumbs and cheese. Cut zucchini in half crosswise; cut each half into 8 sticks. Dip zucchini sticks in egg; dredge in breadcrumb mixture.

2 Pour oil into a Dutch oven or large heavy saucepan to a depth of 2"; heat to 375°. Fry zucchini sticks in hot oil just until coating is golden. Drain on paper towels. Sprinkle with salt, and serve immediately.

"These zucchini 'fries' are a refreshing surprise. I like to serve 'em with warm marinara sauce—they're so-o-o good!"

Soup and Salad Bar

"My hearty soups and salads offer easy, quick, and satisfying solutions for the mealtime doldrums."

Hot Brown Soup

5 servings

¼　cup butter
¼　cup minced onion
¼　cup all-purpose flour
½　teaspoon garlic salt
⅛　teaspoon hot sauce

4　cups milk
1　cup (4 ounces) shredded sharp
　　　Cheddar cheese
½　cup chopped cooked ham
½　cup chopped cooked turkey
Toppings: crumbled bacon, chopped
　　　tomato, chopped fresh parsley

1 Melt butter in a Dutch oven over medium heat. Add onion; sauté until tender. Add flour, garlic salt, and hot sauce; cook 1 minute, stirring constantly.

2 Gradually stir in milk; cook until thickened and bubbly. Reduce heat; stir in cheese until melted. Add ham and turkey; cook until heated, stirring occasionally. (Do not boil.) Serve with desired toppings.

The Sandwich Connection

The name of this soup derives from the famous Louisville, Kentucky, Hot Brown Sandwich. Like its sandwich counterpart, this cheesy soup includes turkey with crumbled bacon and chopped tomatoes on top.

Cheesy Chicken-Corn Soup

7 servings

3   (10¾-ounce) cans cream of
      chicken soup, undiluted
1   (14-ounce) can chicken broth
1   (16-ounce) package frozen whole
      kernel corn
2   cups chopped cooked chicken
1   (10-ounce) can diced tomatoes and
      green chilies
1   (8½-ounce) can cream-style corn
1   (8-ounce) loaf pasteurized prepared
      cheese product
1   clove garlic, minced
¼   teaspoon pepper

1 Stir soup and broth in a Dutch oven until blended; add corn and remaining ingredients, and bring to a boil over medium heat. Reduce heat, and simmer 30 minutes or until smooth, stirring often. Cool.

Freezing Soup

This soup is a good make-ahead choice because it freezes well. Pour soup into an airtight container, and freeze up to 1 month. When you're ready to serve it, thaw it in the fridge 24 hours; warm in a Dutch oven over low heat until thoroughly heated.

Mexican Lime-Chicken Soup

4 servings

⅛ teaspoon ground cloves
¾ teaspoon dried oregano
⅛ teaspoon ground cinnamon
1 (32-ounce) container chicken broth
3 cups cubed cooked chicken
⅓ cup lime juice

Toppings: cubed avocado, lime slices,
     fried tortilla strips, shredded
     Monterey Jack cheese

1 Combine first 6 ingredients in a large saucepan. Bring to a boil; reduce heat, and simmer, uncovered, 2 to 3 minutes.

2 Ladle into individual soup bowls, and serve with desired toppings.

Fried Tortilla Strips

Fried tortilla strips are easy to make and are a great topping for this soup—they make a tasty treat to nibble on, too! Cut 4 (6") corn tortillas into thin strips. Heat oil in a large skillet until hot. Add tortilla strips, and fry 3 to 4 minutes or until crisp. Drain on paper towels.

Baked Potato Soup

8 servings

5	large baking potatoes
¼	cup butter
1	medium onion, chopped
⅓	cup all-purpose flour
1	quart half-and-half
3	cups milk
1	teaspoon salt
⅛	teaspoon ground white pepper
2	cups (8 ounces) shredded Cheddar cheese
8	bacon slices, cooked and crumbled

1 Prick each potato several times with a fork. Microwave 1" apart on paper towels at HIGH 14 minutes or until done, turning and rearranging after 5 minutes. Let cool. Peel potatoes, and coarsely mash with a fork.

2 Melt butter in a Dutch oven over medium heat; add onion, and sauté until tender. Add flour, stirring until smooth. Stir in potatoes, half-and-half, and next 3 ingredients; cook over low heat until thoroughly heated.

3 Top each serving with cheese and bacon.

"Potatoes, cheese, bacon—you've got all the comforts of home cooking in this crowd-pleasin' soup. It's perfect to serve when the gang's over, and guaranteed to take the chill off a cold, wintry day!"

Wildest Rice Soup

10 servings

1   (6.2-ounce) package long-grain and wild rice mix

1   pound bacon, diced

2   cups chopped fresh mushrooms
1   large onion, diced
3¾ cups half-and-half
2½ cups chicken broth
2   (10¾-ounce) cans cream of potato soup, undiluted
1   (8-ounce) loaf pasteurized prepared cheese product, cubed

1 Cook wild rice mix according to package directions, omitting seasoning packet; set rice aside.

2 Cook bacon in a Dutch oven until crisp. Remove bacon, and drain on paper towels, reserving 2 tablespoons drippings in Dutch oven.

3 Sauté mushrooms and onion in drippings until tender; stir in rice, bacon, half-and-half, and remaining ingredients. Cook over medium-low heat until soup is thoroughly heated and cheese melts, stirring constantly.

"Canned soup gives this creamy, sophisticated soup a convenient boost. To add to an already easy and relaxing supper, prepare the soup ahead, and freeze until ready to reheat and serve."

So-Quick Seafood Chowder

5 servings

12 ounces fresh or frozen orange roughy fillets, thawed

½ (24-ounce) package frozen hash browns with onions and peppers
1 cup water

1 (12-ounce) can evaporated milk
1 (10¾-ounce) can cream of potato soup, undiluted
¼ cup bacon bits
2 teaspoons chopped fresh dill or ¾ teaspoon dried dillweed
¼ teaspoon salt
¼ teaspoon pepper
1 (2-ounce) jar diced pimientos, drained

1 Cut fish fillets into 1" pieces.

2 Bring hash browns and 1 cup water to a boil in a large saucepan; reduce heat, cover, and simmer 5 minutes or until tender.

3 Stir in evaporated milk and next 5 ingredients; return to a boil. Add fish and pimientos; cover, reduce heat, and simmer 3 to 5 minutes or until fish flakes easily with a fork. Serve immediately.

Fish Substitute

Any lean, white fish will make a good substitute for orange roughy in this chowder. Use flounder, cod, haddock, or sole.

Fast-Break Chili

10 servings

4½ pounds ground chuck

2 (1¾-ounce) packages chili
    seasoning mix
3 (15-ounce) cans chili beans
3 (15-ounce) cans tomato sauce
1 cup water
1 teaspoon ground red pepper
½ teaspoon salt
¼ teaspoon black pepper
Toppings: shredded Cheddar cheese,
    sour cream, chopped green onions

1 Cook ground chuck in a Dutch oven, stirring until it crumbles and is no longer pink. Drain in a colander, discarding drippings; return ground chuck to Dutch oven.

2 Stir in chili mix and next 6 ingredients. Bring to a boil; reduce heat, and simmer, uncovered, 20 minutes. Serve with desired toppings.

"*With these convenience ingredients, this chili can be put together fast, giving you a break from long hours of kitchen duty! Don't worry if you don't have a crowd to feed 'cause this chili freezes well.*"

Speedy Chicken Stew

6 servings

2   (14-ounce) cans chicken broth
2   chicken bouillon cubes
1   (20-ounce) package frozen creamed
        corn
1   (10-ounce) package frozen baby
        lima beans
1   large baking potato, peeled and
        diced
1   small jalapeño pepper, seeded and
        minced (optional)
½   large onion, diced
⅛   teaspoon ground red pepper
¼   teaspoon dried thyme

3   cups chopped cooked chicken
1   (14½-ounce) can seasoned diced
        tomatoes with garlic, basil, and
        oregano
1   (6-ounce) can tomato paste

1 Combine first 9 ingredients in a Dutch oven. Bring to a boil over medium-high heat, stirring often. Reduce heat, and simmer 15 to 20 minutes or until potatoes and lima beans are tender.

2 Stir in chopped chicken, diced tomatoes, and tomato paste; simmer 10 more minutes.

MEALTIME ✕ MATTERS

Soup's On!—Engage your family in "souper" conversation at the dinner table. Ask who played in the last "souper" bowl or which "souper" hero would they want to be. You get the picture. It'll be a "souper" night!

Mexi-Stew in a Biscuit Bowl

(pictured on page 106)

6 servings

2¼ cups biscuit mix
⅔ cup milk
½ teaspoon ground red pepper

1 pound ground chuck
1 medium onion, chopped
1 medium-size green bell pepper, chopped
2 (14½-ounce) cans Mexican-style stewed tomatoes, undrained
1 (15-ounce) can kidney beans, drained and rinsed
2 teaspoons chili powder

Toppings: sour cream, sliced green onions

"Forget chili bowls, try biscuit bowls! You can either make your own or use a 16-ounce can of jumbo refrigerated biscuits. Just follow the instructions in Step 2 of this recipe. Either way, you'll make a lasting impression with this edible presentation."

1 Preheat the oven to 450°. Stir together first 3 ingredients. Turn dough out onto a surface sprinkled with additional biscuit mix. Shape into a ball; knead 3 or 4 times. Divide into 6 portions.

2 Invert 6 (6-ounce) ovenproof custard cups several inches apart on a rimmed baking sheet. (Or use an inverted muffin pan.) Coat bottoms of cups with nonstick cooking spray. Roll or pat each dough portion into a 6" circle. Place each on a custard cup; press into a bowl shape. Bake at 450° for 10 to 12 minutes. Cool slightly; remove biscuit bowls to a wire rack.

3 Cook ground chuck, onion, and bell pepper in a Dutch oven over medium heat until meat crumbles and is no longer pink; drain. Stir in tomatoes, beans, and chili powder.

4 Bring ground chuck mixture to a boil; cover, reduce heat, and simmer 35 minutes. Spoon into biscuit bowls, and serve with desired toppings.

Quick Greek Salad

(pictured on page 3)

4 to 6 servings

8	plum tomatoes
1	medium cucumber
1	large green bell pepper
1	small onion
1	(12-ounce) jar marinated artichoke heart quarters
¼	cup Greek salad dressing (see tip)
1	bunch green leaf lettuce, torn
8	to 10 pitted ripe olives
¼	cup crumbled feta cheese

Pita wedges (optional)

1 Cut tomatoes into wedges, and seed. Cut cucumber into thin slices; cut pepper into thin strips. Cut onion into slices, and separate into rings.

2 Drain artichoke hearts, reserving ¼ cup marinade.

3 Whisk together ¼ cup reserved artichoke marinade and the dressing in a large bowl. Add cut vegetables, artichokes, lettuce, and olives, tossing to coat. Cover and chill at least 30 minutes. Sprinkle with feta cheese just before serving. Serve with pita wedges, if desired.

"Liven up your weeknight supper with this speedy salad. It goes great with grilled fish or pasta. And don't worry if you don't have Greek dressing on hand—just use Italian dressing."

Broccoli-Raisin Salad

6 servings

1	medium-size red onion
1	(16-ounce) package fresh broccoli florets
1	(3.75-ounce) package sunflower kernels
1	cup golden raisins
1	cup mayonnaise
4	bacon slices, cooked and crumbled
3	tablespoons red wine vinegar

1 Cut onion into thin slices; cut onion slices in half.

2 Stir together onion, broccoli, and remaining ingredients. Cover and chill at least 2 hours before serving.

"You've probably seen lots of versions of this favorite stand-by. That's because it's so-o-o good! The recipe easily doubles to serve 12—perfect for a hungry bunch. For a lighter version, substitute turkey bacon and low-fat mayonnaise."

Ramen Noodle Salad

8 to 10 servings

1 (3-ounce) package ramen noodle
   soup mix

¼ cup butter
1 cup walnuts or pecans, chopped

1 (16-ounce) package fresh broccoli
   florets
1 head romaine lettuce, torn
4 green onions, chopped
1 (8-ounce) bottle sweet-and-sour
   dressing (see tip)

1 Remove seasoning packet from ramen noodles, and reserve for another use. Break noodles into pieces.

2 Melt butter in a large skillet over medium-high heat; add ramen noodles and walnuts, and sauté until lightly browned. Drain on paper towels.

3 Toss together noodle mixture, broccoli, lettuce, and green onions in a large bowl; add ¼ cup dressing, tossing to coat. Serve with remaining dressing.

Sweet-and-Sour Dressing

If you have some extra time, try your hand at my homemade dressing. Otherwise, the bottled version is just dandy!

½ cup vegetable oil
¼ cup sugar
¼ cup red wine vinegar
1 tablespoon soy sauce
½ teaspoon salt
¼ teaspoon pepper

1 Whisk together all ingredients. Store any remaining dressing in the refrigerator. Yield: 1 cup.

Terrific Tortellini Salad

8 to 10 servings

2 (14-ounce) packages frozen
   cheese-filled tortellini

1 green bell pepper, chopped
1 red bell pepper, chopped
1 cucumber, chopped
1 (14-ounce) can artichoke hearts,
   rinsed and drained
1 (8-ounce) bottle Caesar salad
   dressing

1 tomato, cut into wedges

1 Prepare tortellini according to package directions; drain. Rinse with cold water; drain.

2 Combine tortellini, peppers, and next 3 ingredients in a large bowl; cover and chill 2 hours.

3 Arrange tomato wedges over salad just before serving.

"This salad is terrific because it's great tastin', quick, and can be made as much as 8 hours ahead! The flavors only get better the longer it chills."

Greek Potato Salad

5 cups

2	pounds new potatoes
¼	cup olive oil
¼	cup red wine vinegar
3	tablespoons mayonnaise
½	teaspoon salt
½	teaspoon dried oregano
½	teaspoon pepper
½	cup pitted kalamata olives
1	(4-ounce) package crumbled feta cheese
3	green bell pepper slices

1 Place potatoes in a Dutch oven; add salted water to cover, and boil 30 minutes. Cool slightly. Cut into 1" pieces.

2 Whisk together oil and next 5 ingredients; toss with potatoes.

3 Sprinkle with olives and feta cheese. Top with bell pepper slices for garnish.

MEALTIME ✕ MATTERS

Teach and Cook—Involve your kids in mealtime preparation by having them read the recipe aloud as you prepare it. Talk about where different foods come from, or how a recipe got its name. For example, what makes this potato salad Greek? Think kalamata olives, feta cheese, and oregano!

Tea-riffic Spiced Fruit Salad

2¼ cups

¼   cup sugar
¼   cup water
1   orange-and-spice tea bag

1   cup fresh orange sections
1   cup fresh grapefruit sections
1   cup cubed fresh pineapple

1 Bring sugar and water to a boil in a small saucepan; boil until sugar dissolves, stirring constantly. Remove from heat, and add tea bag; cover and steep 5 minutes. Remove tea bag, squeezing gently. Cool tea mixture.

2 Toss together fruit and tea mixture. Cover and chill 8 hours before serving.

MEALTIME ✕ MATTERS

Breakfast, Anyone?—Get the day off to a great start with the ultimate morning indulgence of breakfast in bed! Recognize a birthday, anniversary, or the first or *last* day of school with a breakfast of the honoree's favorite foods.

Banana Split Salad

15 servings

1   (8-ounce) package cream cheese,
    softened
½   cup sugar

1   (20-ounce) can crushed pineapple
    in juice, drained
1   (10-ounce) package frozen
    strawberries in syrup, thawed
    and undrained
2   medium bananas, coarsely chopped
1   (12-ounce) container frozen
    whipped topping, thawed
1   cup chopped walnuts

1 Combine cream cheese and sugar in a mixing bowl; beat at medium speed of an electric beater until blended.

2 Stir in pineapple, strawberries, and bananas. Gently fold in whipped topping and walnuts.

3 Pour mixture into an ungreased 9" x 13" dish. Cover and freeze 8 hours. Let stand at room temperature 30 minutes before serving.

"Kids will love this dessertlike salad. Serve it as an accompaniment with your entrée or as the meal's finale—either way, they'll keep comin' back for more."

Creamy Coleslaw

5 cups

1   (16-ounce) jar coleslaw dressing
½   cup dill pickle juice
½   teaspoon celery seeds (optional)
2   (16-ounce) packages coleslaw mix

1 Stir together dressing, pickle juice, and celery seeds, if desired, in a large bowl; add coleslaw mix, tossing to coat. Chill at least 1 hour before serving.

MEALTIME MATTERS

Picnic Fun—Don't let inclement weather spoil your picnic plans—bring the gang inside! Spread a quilt on the floor with all the goodies on top, play board games in place of ball games, and don't forget the marshmallows for toasting in the fireplace.

Herbed Salad Dressing Mix

¾ cup

½   cup dried parsley flakes
¼   cup freeze-dried chives
1   tablespoon dried dillweed
¼   teaspoon salt
⅛   teaspoon pepper

1 Stir together all ingredients, and store in an airtight container up to 6 months. Use as directed below.

Herbed Salad Dressing

To make dressing, whisk together 2 tablespoons Herbed Salad Dressing Mix, ½ cup mayonnaise, and ½ cup buttermilk or sour cream. Chill at least 2 hours. Serve over mixed salad greens or as a vegetable dip. Yield: 1 cup.

Vinaigrette Salad Dressing

1 ½ cups

½ cup apple cider vinegar
3 tablespoons chopped onion
2½ tablespoons sugar
1 large clove garlic
1 teaspoon salt
1 teaspoon dry mustard
½ teaspoon pepper

1 cup vegetable oil

1 Process first 7 ingredients in a blender until smooth.

2 With blender running, add oil in a slow, steady stream; process until smooth. Cover and chill.

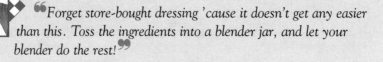

Forget store-bought dressing 'cause it doesn't get any easier than this. Toss the ingredients into a blender jar, and let your blender do the rest!

Breadshoppe Bounty

66Easy to make and fast to bake is how I describe the down-home goodness of these breads!99

Quick Whipping Cream Biscuits

1 dozen

½   cup butter
2   cups self-rising flour
¾   to 1 cup whipping cream

¼   cup butter, melted

1 Preheat the oven to 400°. Cut ½ cup butter into flour with a pastry blender or fork until crumbly. Add whipping cream, stirring just until dry ingredients are moistened.

2 Turn dough out onto a lightly floured surface, and knead lightly 3 or 4 times. Roll or pat dough to ¾" thickness. Cut with a 2" round cutter; place biscuits on a lightly greased baking sheet.

3 Bake at 400° for 13 to 15 minutes. Brush biscuits with ¼ cup melted butter.

Fast Finger Work!

If you'd rather not bother with a rolling pin, you can pat the dough with your fingers onto a floured surface to about ¾" thickness. To keep the dough from sticking to your biscuit cutter, just dip the cutter in flour.

English Cheese Muffins

8 servings

8   bacon slices, cooked and crumbled
1   (5-ounce) jar sharp process cheese
       spread
¼   cup butter, softened
1   green onion, chopped
4   English muffins, split

Sliced tomato (optional)

1 Preheat the oven to 325°. Stir together first 4 ingredients; spread about 2 tablespoons cheese mixture on each muffin half.

2 Bake at 325° for 15 minutes or until golden. Serve with sliced tomato, if desired.

MEALTIME MATTERS

Butter Up!—Add some of your favorite preserves or jam to softened butter, and stir until blended. Serve with English muffins or biscuits for a flavor-packed breakfast spread.

Mini Orange-Date Muffins

4 dozen

1   (1-pound, 6-ounce) package date
      quick bread-and-muffin mix
1   tablespoon grated orange rind
1   large egg, lightly beaten
1   cup orange juice
½   cup butter, melted

1 Preheat the oven to 400°. Stir together all ingredients; spoon batter into lightly greased miniature (1¾") muffin pans, filling two-thirds full.

2 Bake in batches at 400° for 10 to 12 minutes or until golden. Remove muffins from pans immediately, and cool on wire racks.

MEALTIME MATTERS

Bounty of Bread—Brighten a friend's day with a basket of muffins. For an added touch, place a tea towel in the bottom of the basket. And how nice to greet new neighbors with a loaf of homemade bread. Wrap it in cellophane or plastic wrap, and tie with a colorful bow for a welcoming gift.

White Chocolate-Macadamia Muffins

1 dozen

2½ cups biscuit mix
½ cup sugar
¾ cup coarsely chopped white
  chocolate
½ cup coarsely chopped macadamia
  nuts

¾ cup half-and-half
3 tablespoons vegetable oil
2 teaspoons vanilla extract
1 large egg, lightly beaten

1 Preheat the oven to 400°. Combine biscuit mix and sugar in a large bowl; stir in chocolate and nuts. Make a well in center of mixture.

2 Combine half-and-half and remaining 3 ingredients; pour into well of biscuit mix mixture, stirring just until moistened.

3 Spoon into greased muffin pans, filling two-thirds full. Bake at 400° for 11 to 12 minutes or until a wooden toothpick inserted in center comes out clean. Remove from pans immediately.

More Muffins

Hot Cocoa Muffins: Omit white chocolate and macadamia nuts. Reduce biscuit mix to 2¼ cups and half-and-half to ½ cup. Stir in 2 tablespoons unsweetened cocoa, ¾ cup semisweet mini chocolate chips, ¼ cup chocolate flavor syrup, and ¼ cup sliced almonds. Bake as directed. Yield: 1 dozen.

Ham and Cheese Muffins: Omit sugar, chocolate, nuts, and vanilla. Add ¾ cup diced ham (for maximum flavor, use country ham) and ¾ cup shredded sharp Cheddar cheese. Bake as directed. Yield: 1 dozen.

Classic Cream Scones

1 dozen

2   cups all-purpose flour
2   teaspoons baking powder
⅛   teaspoon salt
¼   cup sugar
⅓   cup butter, cubed

½   cup whipping cream
1   large egg
1½   teaspoons vanilla extract

1   egg white
1   teaspoon water
Additional sugar

1 Preheat the oven to 425°. Combine first 4 ingredients. Cut in butter with a pastry blender or fork until crumbly.

2 Whisk together cream, egg, and vanilla; add to flour mixture, stirring just until moistened.

3 Turn dough out onto a lightly floured surface. Pat dough to ½" thickness; cut with a 2½" round cutter, and place on baking sheets.

4 Whisk together egg white and 1 teaspoon water; brush mixture over scones. Sprinkle scones with additional sugar. Bake at 425° for 13 to 15 minutes or until lightly browned.

"I think you'll agree when I say these scones are some of the best ever! And they take only 25 minutes from start to finish—ooh they're so good!"

Mama's Mini-Cinnis

(pictured on page 107)

2 dozen

2   (8-ounce) cans refrigerated crescent rolls

6   tablespoons butter, softened
⅓   cup packed brown sugar
1   tablespoon granulated sugar
1   teaspoon ground cinnamon
¼   cup chopped pecans

1⅓   cups sifted powdered sugar
2   tablespoons milk
¼   teaspoon vanilla extract

1 Preheat the oven to 375°. Unroll crescent rolls, and separate each dough portion along center perforation to form 4 rectangles; press diagonal perforations to seal.

2 Stir together butter and next 3 ingredients; spread evenly over 1 side of each rectangle. Sprinkle with pecans. Roll up jellyroll fashion, starting at long end. (See tip.) Gently cut each log into 6 (1"-thick) slices, using a serrated knife. Place rolls, ¼" apart, into 2 (8") greased cakepans, placing 3 in the center.

3 Bake at 375° for 15 to 17 minutes or until golden. Remove from pans. Cool 5 to 10 minutes.

4 Stir together powdered sugar, milk, and vanilla; drizzle over warm rolls.

Slicing Tip
To make slicing easier, place unbaked rolls on a baking sheet, and freeze 10 minutes. You can easily double this recipe for a crowd.

139

Orange Pancakes with Sunshine Orange Sauce

14 (4") pancakes

2   cups biscuit mix
3   tablespoons sugar

2   large eggs
¾   cup orange juice
¾   cup milk

Sunshine Orange Sauce
    (see recipe below)

1 Combine biscuit mix and sugar in a large bowl; make a well in center of mixture.

2 Combine eggs, orange juice, and milk in a small bowl, stirring well; pour into well of biscuit mix mixture, stirring just until moistened.

3 Pour ¼ cup batter for each pancake onto a hot, lightly greased griddle. Cook pancakes until tops are covered with bubbles and edges appear cooked; turn and cook other side. Serve with warm Sunshine Orange Sauce.

Sunshine Orange Sauce

¼   cup sugar
1½   teaspoons cornstarch
¾   cup orange juice

1 Bring all ingredients to a boil in a small saucepan over medium heat, stirring constantly; boil 1 minute. Yield: ¾ cup.

"Your morning orange juice is already in these pancakes, so enjoy them with a glass of cold milk instead."

Stuffed French Toast

8 servings

½   (8-ounce) package cream cheese, softened
⅓   cup chopped pecans, toasted
4   teaspoons orange marmalade

2   French bread loaves, cut diagonally into 8 (1"-thick) slices

4   large eggs
1   cup milk
1   teaspoon ground cinnamon

3   tablespoons butter
2   tablespoons powdered sugar

1 Stir together cream cheese, chopped pecans, and orange marmalade.

2 Cut a horizontal pocket into top crust of each bread slice. Spoon about 2 teaspoons cream cheese mixture into each pocket.

3 Whisk together eggs, milk, and cinnamon; dip stuffed bread slices into mixture, coating all sides.

4 Melt butter in a large nonstick skillet over medium-high heat. Cook stuffed bread slices, in batches, 2 minutes on each side or until golden. Sprinkle with powdered sugar. Serve with your favorite syrup.

"What's better than waking up to comforting French toast right out of the skillet? How 'bout thick slices of French toast stuffed with orange marmalade, cream cheese, and pecans! Don't forget the syrup!"

Cheesy Garlic Bread

8 slices

½ cup butter
4 cloves garlic, pressed
½ teaspoon salt

1 (16-ounce) Italian bread loaf

1½ teaspoons Italian seasoning
½ cup freshly grated Parmesan cheese

1 Melt butter in a skillet over medium-high heat; add garlic and salt, and sauté 2 minutes.

2 Preheat the oven to Broil. Cut bread into 1½" slices, and dip into butter mixture, coating both sides. Place on a baking sheet.

3 Stir together Italian seasoning and Parmesan cheese; sprinkle on 1 side of each bread slice.

4 Broil 5½" from heat 4 minutes or until cheese melts.

MEALTIME MATTERS

Worldly Meals—Once a month—or week—have a family member highlight a country from around the world to talk about at dinnertime. Ask them to search for customs and foods that are native to that country. Plan a meal from the featured country and have the family member talk about their worldly finds.

Spicy Breadsticks

6 servings

1   (11-ounce) can refrigerated
     breadstick dough
1   large egg, lightly beaten

2   tablespoons paprika
2   tablespoons seasoned pepper
     (see tip)

1 Preheat the oven to 375°. Separate breadsticks; working with 2 at a time, roll each breadstick into a 20" rope. Brush ropes with egg. Twist ropes together, pinching ends to seal. Repeat with remaining breadsticks.

2 Combine paprika and pepper; spread mixture on a rimmed baking sheet. Roll breadsticks in pepper mixture, pressing gently to coat.

3 Place breadsticks on a greased baking sheet, and bake at 375° for 10 minutes.

"These spicy hot breadsticks are perfect companions for gumbo, stew, or chili. If you can't find seasoned pepper, combine equal portions of cracked black pepper, sweet red pepper flakes, and salt."

Hot-Water Cornbread

1 dozen

2   cups white cornmeal
¼   teaspoon baking powder
1 ¼ teaspoons salt
1   teaspoon sugar
¼   cup half-and-half
1   tablespoon vegetable oil
¾   to 1 ¼ cups boiling water
    (see note)

Vegetable oil
Softened butter

1 Combine first 4 ingredients in a bowl; stir in half-and-half and 1 tablespoon oil. Gradually add boiling water, stirring until batter is the consistency of oatmeal.

2 Pour oil into a large heavy skillet to a depth of ½"; place over medium-high heat. Scoop batter into a ¼-cup measure; drop into hot oil, and fry in batches 3 minutes on each side or until golden. Drain on paper towels. Serve with softened butter.

Note: The amount of boiling water needed varies depending on the type of cornmeal used. Stone-ground (coarsely ground) cornmeal requires more liquid.

Pick Your Favorite!

Country Ham Hot-Water Cornbread: After adding boiling water, stir in 1 ½ cups finely chopped cooked country ham.

Bacon-Cheddar Hot-Water Cornbread: After adding boiling water, stir in 8 slices crumbled, cooked bacon, 1 cup shredded sharp Cheddar cheese, and 4 minced green onions.

Southwestern Hot-Water Cornbread: After adding boiling water, stir in 1 jalapeño pepper, seeded and minced; 1 cup shredded Mexican cheese blend; 1 cup frozen whole kernel corn, thawed; and ¼ cup minced fresh cilantro.

Corn Soufflé Hush Puppies

4 dozen

2   (12-ounce) packages frozen corn
       soufflé

1½   cups self-rising flour
1½   cups cornmeal
½   to 1 teaspoon ground red pepper
½   cup chopped onion
1   large egg
¾   cup plus 2 tablespoons milk
3   tablespoons vegetable oil

Vegetable oil

1 Thaw corn soufflé in microwave at MEDIUM (50% power) 6 to 7 minutes, stirring once.

2 Combine flour and next 3 ingredients in a medium bowl. Combine egg, milk, and 3 tablespoons oil; stir into flour mixture. Fold in corn soufflé.

3 Pour oil into a Dutch oven to a depth of 2"; heat to 370°. (See tip on page 81.) Drop batter by tablespoonfuls into hot oil. Fry 3 to 5 minutes or until golden, turning once. Drain on paper towels.

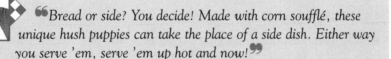

Bread or side? You decide! Made with corn soufflé, these unique hush puppies can take the place of a side dish. Either way you serve 'em, serve 'em up hot and now!

Herbed Fan-Tan Dinner Rolls

1 dozen

¼ cup butter, melted
½ teaspoon dried Italian seasoning

1 (17.4-ounce) package refrigerated
  loaf bread

1 Combine butter and Italian seasoning, stirring well.

2 Roll dough into an 8" x 15" rectangle. Cut into 4 (2"-wide) lengthwise strips. Stack strips on top of each other. Cut strips crosswise into 12 equal pieces.

3 Place each piece, cut side up, into greased muffin pans; brush with butter mixture. Cover and let rise in a warm place (85°), free from drafts, 25 minutes or until doubled in bulk.

4 Preheat the oven to 375°. Bake at 375° for 20 minutes or until golden. Brush with butter mixture again, if desired.

"When baked, the layers in this tan-colored roll spread out to mimic a fan—hence the name 'fan-tan'! These rolls are great to make ahead. Place dough pieces in muffin pans; brush with butter mixture. Cover and freeze. Thaw, covered, in a warm place, 2 hours or until doubled. Bake as directed."

Bacon Monkey Bread

1 (10") ring

11 bacon slices, cooked and crumbled
½ cup grated Parmesan cheese
1 small onion, chopped

3 (10-ounce) cans refrigerated
buttermilk biscuits
½ cup butter, melted

1 Preheat the oven to 350°. Combine first 3 ingredients, and set aside.

2 Cut each biscuit into fourths. Dip one-third of biscuit pieces into melted butter, and place in a lightly greased 12-cup Bundt pan. Sprinkle with half of bacon mixture. Repeat layers with remaining biscuit pieces and bacon mixture, ending with biscuit pieces.

3 Bake at 350° for 40 minutes or until golden. Cool in pan 10 minutes; invert onto a serving platter, and serve bread immediately.

"Monkey bread can be savory or sweet. What's unique about it is that you pull it apart to serve instead of slicing it. It's best served warm—so have at it!"

Quick Flatbread

4 to 6 servings

1   (10-ounce) can refrigerated pizza
    crust
¼   cup olive oil, divided

1   large sweet onion
2   cloves garlic, minced
1½ teaspoons dried Italian seasoning
⅛   teaspoon salt
¼   teaspoon pepper

¾   cup (3 ounces) shredded Asiago or
    Parmesan cheese

1 Preheat the oven to 425°. Unroll pizza crust; place on a baking sheet. Press handle of a wooden spoon into crust to make indentations at 1" intervals; brush crust with 2 tablespoons olive oil. Bake at 425° for 10 to 12 minutes.

2 Cut onion into thin slices; cut each slice in half. Sauté onion in remaining 2 tablespoons olive oil over medium heat about 8 minutes or until browned. Add garlic and next 3 ingredients, and sauté 1 minute.

3 Top pizza crust with onion mixture, and sprinkle with cheese. Bake at 425° for 5 minutes or until cheese is melted. Serve immediately.

"Commercial pizza dough is the secret to this quick flat-bread. Serve it with your favorite soup or salad for a tasty combo."

Pesto Provolone Batter Bread

10 servings

1 (16-ounce) package hot roll mix, yeast packet reserved
½ cup plus 2 tablespoons (2.5 ounces) shredded provolone cheese, divided
1¼ cups hot water (120° to 130°)
1 large egg
1 (3.5-ounce) jar prepared pesto sauce

1 tablespoon pine nuts

1 Combine roll mix, yeast packet, and ½ cup cheese in a large mixing bowl, stirring well. Add hot water and egg, beating 2 minutes at medium speed of a heavy-duty electric stand mixer. (See tip.) Add pesto, beating well.

2 Scrape dough from sides of bowl. Cover and let rise in a warm place (85°), free from drafts, 30 minutes or until doubled in bulk. Stir dough 25 strokes with a wooden spoon.

3 Preheat the oven to 350°. Spoon batter into a greased 2-quart round casserole; sprinkle with pine nuts.

4 Sprinkle batter with remaining 2 tablespoons cheese. Bake at 350° for 45 minutes or until loaf sounds hollow when tapped.

"You'll need to get out your heavy-duty mixer for this succulent bread, folks. The batter tends to ride up the beaters if you use a regular mixer. But once you taste this bread, you'll definitely think it was worth the effort! And if you like to make your own pesto, substitute about ⅓ cup for the jar of pesto."

Lemon-Swirled Gingerbread

9 servings

2   (3-ounce) packages cream cheese,
      softened
¼   cup granulated sugar
1   large egg
½   cup lemon curd

1   (10-ounce) package gingerbread
      mix
2   teaspoons powdered sugar

1 Beat cream cheese at medium speed of an electric beater until smooth. Gradually add ¼ cup sugar, beating well. Add egg, beating just until blended. Fold in lemon curd.

2 Preheat the oven to 350°. Prepare gingerbread batter according to package directions. Pour half of batter into a greased 8" square pan. Dollop lemon mixture over batter; pour remaining batter over lemon mixture. Swirl a knife through batter, touching bottom of pan and swirling to bring some lemon mixture to top of cake. Bake at 350° for 35 minutes or until a knife inserted in center comes out clean. Cool in pan on a wire rack. Sift powdered sugar over cake.

"This recipe is super-easy to prepare, especially with gingerbread mix and store-bought lemon curd. People will think you spent hours in the kitchen! You can find already prepared lemon curd in the jams and jellies section of most supermarkets."

Caramel-Nut Pull-Apart Bread

12 servings

1   cup plus 2 tablespoons packed
      brown sugar
1   cup chopped walnuts
¾   cup butter, melted

3   (10-ounce) cans refrigerated biscuits

1 Preheat the oven to 350°. Combine brown sugar and walnuts in a small bowl; stir in butter. Spoon half of sugar mixture into a greased 12-cup Bundt pan.

2 Cut each biscuit in half (use kitchen scissors for quick cutting). Place half of biscuit halves over sugar mixture. Spoon remaining sugar mixture over biscuits in pan; top with remaining biscuits. Bake at 350° for 30 to 35 minutes or until browned. Turn out onto a serving platter immediately, spooning any sauce left in pan over bread.

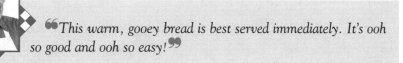

"This warm, gooey bread is best served immediately. It's ooh so good and ooh so easy!"

Pecan Crescent Twists

8 servings

2 (8-ounce) cans refrigerated crescent rolls
3 tablespoons butter, melted and divided

½ cup chopped pecans
¼ cup granulated sugar
1 teaspoon ground cinnamon
⅛ teaspoon ground nutmeg

½ cup powdered sugar
2½ teaspoons maple syrup

1 Preheat the oven to 375°. Unroll crescent rolls, and separate each can into 2 rectangles, pressing perforations to seal. Brush evenly with 2 tablespoons melted butter.

2 Stir together chopped pecans and next 3 ingredients; sprinkle 3 tablespoons pecan mixture onto each rectangle, pressing in gently.

3 Roll up, starting at 1 long side, and twist. Cut 6 shallow ½"-long diagonal slits in each roll. Shape rolls into rings, pressing ends together; place on a lightly greased baking sheet. Brush rings evenly with remaining 1 tablespoon butter.

4 Bake at 375° for 12 minutes or until rings are golden.

5 Meanwhile, stir together powdered sugar and maple syrup until glaze is smooth; drizzle over warm rings. Cut rings in half, and serve.

MEALTIME MATTERS

Bread Twists—Make bread the center of your table—literally! Placed in vases, breadsticks make attractive and edible centerpieces. Try stacking rolls on graduated cake stands for an equally unique focal point.

Sweet Inspiration

66Sink your teeth into these sinfully delicious treats that are fit for any occasion!99

Caramel-Toffee Bombe

4 to 6 servings

¾ cup gingersnap cookie crumbs
    (about 10 cookies)
2   tablespoons butter, melted

1   pint vanilla ice cream, softened
2   (1.4-ounce) chocolate-covered
    toffee candy bars, crushed

1   (12-ounce) jar caramel sauce

1 Line a 2-quart bowl with heavy-duty plastic wrap. Stir together cookie crumbs and butter; press mixture into prepared bowl.

2 Stir together ice cream and candy; spoon over crumbs. Cover and freeze 8 hours.

3 Invert bowl onto a serving plate. Carefully remove bowl and plastic wrap. Cut into wedges, and serve immediately with warm caramel sauce.

MEALTIME ✕ MATTERS

Flower Power—Brighten up your table by adding colorful flowers that will last all week. And you don't have to visit your local florist for beautiful fresh flowers. Check out the wonderful selection at your supermarket for inexpensive selections that you can mix and match.

Toffee Crunch Ice Cream Balls

4 servings

2   cups coffee ice cream
3   (1.4-ounce) chocolate-covered
       toffee candy bars, crushed

4   waffle cone bowls
Chocolate ice cream topping

1 Scoop ice cream into 4 balls; place on a wax paper-lined baking sheet, and freeze until firm. Roll ice cream balls in crushed candy; freeze until firm.

2 To serve, place ice cream balls in waffle bowls; drizzle with chocolate topping.

"Try your own combination of ice cream flavors, coatings, and toppings for endless variations of this easy, yet fancy, dessert."

Dessert Tacos

4 servings

1   tablespoon sugar
¼   teaspoon ground cinnamon
4   (8") flour tortillas
1   tablespoon butter, melted

2   cups chocolate ice cream
2   kiwifruit, peeled and cut into strips
1   pint strawberries, sliced
1   cup frozen whipped topping,
        thawed

How 'bout tacos for dessert? Load 'em up with ice cream, fresh fruit, and a dollop of whipped cream, and watch everybody come runnin' to the table!

1 Preheat the oven to 350°. Combine sugar and cinnamon. Brush tortillas with melted butter; sprinkle evenly with sugar mixture.

2 Shape 4 sheets of aluminum foil into 4" balls on a baking sheet. Place tortillas, butter side down, on foil; press to resemble taco shells.

3 Bake at 350° for 10 minutes or until crisp. Cool completely on foil on baking sheet.

4 Remove tortillas from baking sheet; fill evenly with ice cream, kiwifruit, and strawberries. Dollop with whipped topping.

Lemon Ice

4 cups

1   (12-ounce) can frozen lemonade
    concentrate, thawed and undiluted
3   cups ice cubes
1   cup water
⅓   cup sugar

1 Process all ingredients in a food
processor or blender until smooth.
Pour mixture into a 9" x 13" pan, and
freeze 45 minutes.

2 Process frozen mixture in a food
processor or blender until smooth.
Return to pan, and freeze 8 more hours.

*"Take time to chill with this easy make-ahead dessert! With
dessert already made, you can savor the evening and make at
least part of your weeknight meal less hectic."*

Hot Fudge Ice-Cream Topping

1½ cups

2   (1-ounce) squares semisweet
      baking chocolate
1   cup evaporated milk
¾   cup sugar

2   tablespoons butter
1   teaspoon vanilla extract

1 Cook first 3 ingredients in a saucepan over low heat 6 minutes or until chocolate melts and mixture is smooth, stirring constantly.

2 Bring chocolate mixture to a boil over medium heat. Boil 6 minutes, stirring constantly. Remove from heat; stir in butter and vanilla. Serve warm over ice cream. Store, covered, in refrigerator up to 3 weeks.

"*With a batch of this favorite topper in the fridge and ice cream in the freezer, you'll have dessert on a moment's notice.* 'OH IT'S SO GOOD!!'"

Apple-Blueberry Crunch

8 to 10 servings

1   (21-ounce) can apple pie filling

1   (14-ounce) package frozen
        blueberries
1   cup sugar, divided
1   (18.25-ounce) package white cake
        mix
½   cup butter, melted
1   cup chopped walnuts, toasted

Ice cream or whipped topping

1 Preheat the oven to 350°. Spread apple pie filling in a lightly greased 9" x 13" pan.

2 Toss together frozen blueberries and ¾ cup sugar; spoon over apple pie filling. Sprinkle cake mix evenly over fruit, and drizzle with melted butter. Sprinkle with chopped walnuts and remaining ¼ cup sugar.

3 Bake at 350° for 45 to 50 minutes or until golden and bubbly. Serve with ice cream or whipped topping.

Mix It Up!

Mix and match these ingredients according to the preparations in the above recipe. Or get creative, and use this list to brainstorm even more possibilities!

Frozen fruit: blueberries, raspberries, sliced strawberries

Canned pie fillings: apple, cherry, peach, blueberry, strawberry

Cake mixes: yellow, white, chocolate, spice, strawberry

Toasted nuts (chopped or slivered): pecans, walnuts, peanuts, almonds

Toppings: milk chocolate chips, semisweet chocolate chips, white chocolate chips, sweetened flaked coconut, cinnamon

Peach-of-a-Dish

6 servings

3   (15-ounce) cans peach halves in
     heavy syrup, drained
¼   cup packed brown sugar
1   teaspoon ground cinnamon
Dash of ground nutmeg
3   tablespoons butter, cut into pieces

1 Preheat the oven to 325°. Place peach halves in a 7" x 11" baking dish. Sprinkle with brown sugar, cinnamon, and nutmeg; dot with butter. Bake, uncovered, at 325° for 45 minutes.

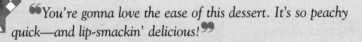

"You're gonna love the ease of this dessert. It's so peachy quick—and lip-smackin' delicious!"

Cinnamon Apple Dumplings

8 servings

¼ cup butter

¼ cup granulated sugar
¼ cup water

1 (8-ounce) package refrigerated
crescent rolls

1⅓ cups apple pie filling, coarsely
chopped, or 1 (12-ounce) package
frozen apple chunks, thawed
¼ cup packed light brown sugar
2 tablespoons all-purpose flour
¼ teaspoon ground cinnamon
½ cup chopped pecans, toasted

1 Melt butter in a 7" x 11" baking dish; set aside.

2 Cook granulated sugar and ¼ cup water in a saucepan over medium heat until sugar melts; set aside.

3 Preheat the oven to 350°. Roll crescent roll dough into a 10" x 14" rectangle.

4 Combine apples, brown sugar, and remaining 3 ingredients. Spread over dough to within ½" of edges. Starting with short end, roll dough up, jellyroll fashion, pressing seam to seal; cut into 16 (¾"-thick) slices, and place in baking dish. Pour sugar mixture carefully over dumplings. Bake at 350° for 35 to 38 minutes or until golden.

❝Dental floss is the utensil of choice for cutting this soft dough. Just place a 10" piece of floss under the dough, and cross the two strands over the top to cut a slice. And don't let that leftover pie filling go to waste. Use the extra as a topping for pancakes, waffles, French toast, or even ice cream!❞

Taffy Apple Pizza

16 servings

½   cup water
1   tablespoon lemon juice
5   medium Braeburn or Fuji apples,
     peeled and thinly sliced

1   (20-ounce) package refrigerated
     sugar cookie dough

2   (8-ounce) packages cream cheese,
     softened
1   cup packed brown sugar
1   teaspoon vanilla extract

¼   cup caramel topping

1 Preheat the oven to 350°. Combine water and lemon juice in a medium bowl; add apple slices.

2 Press cookie dough evenly onto an ungreased 12" pizza pan. Bake at 350° for 15 minutes or until golden. Cool crust in pan on a wire rack.

3 Beat cream cheese, brown sugar, and vanilla at medium speed of an electric beater until smooth. Spread over cookie crust.

4 Drain apple slices; arrange over cream cheese layer. Drizzle with caramel topping, slice, and serve.

"Treat your family to pizza for dessert! They'll love the sugar cookie crust that's layered with gooey cream cheese and warm apples. And don't forget to top it off with your favorite caramel sauce. It's a real crowd-pleaser!"

Mocha Dessert Squares

9 servings

2	cups whipping cream
3	tablespoons chocolate flavor sauce
1	tablespoon instant coffee granules
1	teaspoon vanilla extract
¾	cup sifted powdered sugar
27	graham cracker squares

1 Pour whipping cream into a medium bowl. Add chocolate sauce, coffee granules, and vanilla, stirring until coffee granules dissolve. Beat whipping cream mixture at medium speed of an electric beater until foamy; gradually add powdered sugar, beating until soft peaks form.

2 Place 9 graham cracker squares in an 8" square pan. Spread ⅓ of cream mixture over crackers. Repeat layers twice with remaining ingredients. Cover and chill at least 8 hours. Serve with additional chocolate sauce, if desired.

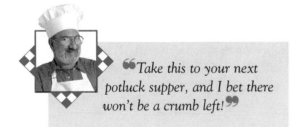

❝Take this to your next potluck supper, and I bet there won't be a crumb left!❞

Indoor S'Mores

6 servings

1	(4.6-ounce) package vanilla pudding mix
8	graham cracker sheets (32 cookies)
4	(1.55-ounce) milk chocolate candy bars
¾	cup mini marshmallows

1 Cook pudding according to package directions.

2 Preheat the oven to 350°. Arrange 4 graham cracker sheets in an 8" square pan. Top with 2 candy bars and ½ of pudding. Repeat layers. Sprinkle with mini marshmallows.

3 Bake at 350° for 10 minutes or until lightly browned.

"Have s'mores indoors! They're really easy to make following my simple recipe. I've included all the traditional ingredients—plus pudding. Serve this treat, and there's sure to be smiles all around your campfire...I mean your dinner table!"

Individual Raspberry Trifles

4 servings

1 (3.9-ounce) package vanilla instant pudding mix

2 cups fresh raspberries or 2 cups individually frozen unsweetened raspberries, thawed and drained

½ cup seedless raspberry jam

½ (10.75-ounce) pound cake, cut into ½" cubes

½ cup whipping cream
1 tablespoon sugar

1 Prepare pudding according to package directions.

2 Stir together raspberries and jam. Spoon ¼ cup raspberry mixture equally into 4 martini glasses. (See tip.)

3 Top with ¼ cup pudding and then equal amounts of pound cake. Spoon remaining raspberry mixture over cake; top with remaining pudding. Chill, if desired.

4 Beat whipping cream and sugar at high speed of an electric beater until soft peaks form. Dollop on trifles.

66Dust off your martini glasses, but hold the ice! The shapely beverage glasses beautifully display this easy-yet-elegant dessert. If you don't have any martini glasses, just use a similar size glass or dessert dish.99

Chocolate Pots de Crème

4 to 6 servings

1 cup (6 ounces) semisweet chocolate
   chips
1 cup whipping cream
½ cup half-and-half

2 egg yolks

Pots de Crème is a fancy French dessert of creamy pudding that's often served in special little porcelain cups or tiny pots with lids. My version boasts just 4 ingredients and requires only a saucepan and a few utensils.

1 Combine first 3 ingredients in a heavy saucepan; cook over low heat until chocolate melts, stirring constantly.

2 Beat egg yolks until thick and pale. Gradually stir about ¼ of hot mixture into yolks; add to remaining hot mixture in saucepan, stirring constantly.

3 Cook over low heat 2 minutes or until mixture thickens slightly, stirring constantly. Spoon into individual pots de crème cups or custard cups. Cover and chill.

No-Bake Banana Pudding Delight

6 servings

1	(3.4-ounce) package vanilla instant pudding mix
½	cup sour cream
1¾	cups milk

48	vanilla wafers
2	medium bananas, sliced

Frozen whipped topping, thawed

1 Beat first 3 ingredients at low speed of an electric beater 2 minutes or until thickened.

2 Line bottom and sides of a 1½-quart bowl with vanilla wafers. Layer with ⅓ of pudding mixture and ½ of the bananas; repeat layers, ending with pudding mixture. Chill. Spread with whipped topping.

MEALTIME MATTERS

Just Dessert—If dessert's your thing, invite the gang over for a dessert party. You'll want to plan for a later time than usual so it won't conflict with dinnertime. Serve up a variety of your favorite sweets—plus coffee. This is a great way to entertain without planning a complete meal.

Ice Cream Angel Squares

6 servings

2   teaspoons instant coffee granules
2   teaspoons hot water

½   cup butter, softened
2   cups sifted powdered sugar

1   (10½-ounce) angel food cake loaf
1   (3.5-ounce) jar macadamia nuts,
       chopped (see tip)
1   quart vanilla ice cream
¾   to 1 cup chocolate sauce
¾   to 1 cup caramel sauce

1 Dissolve coffee granules in 2 teaspoons hot water.

2 Beat butter at medium speed of an electric beater until creamy; gradually add sugar, beating until light and fluffy. Add coffee, and beat until spreading consistency.

3 Trim crust from cake. Cut cake into 6 (2½" x 1") squares. Spread frosting on top and sides of squares; roll in nuts. Top with ice cream, and drizzle with sauces.

"I love the rich, buttery flavor that the macadamia nuts give to this angelic dessert, but dry-roasted peanuts will work just as well. You'll want to use ¾ cup of chopped peanuts in place of the jar of macadamia nuts."

German Chocolate Snack Cake

18 squares

1   (18.25-ounce) package German
     chocolate cake mix
4   large eggs
½   cup chopped pecans, toasted
½   cup butter, melted

1   (16-ounce) package powdered
     sugar
1   (8-ounce) package cream cheese,
     softened

Ice cream or whipped topping

1 Preheat the oven to 300°. Stir together cake mix, 1 egg, the pecans, and butter; press mixture into a lightly greased 9" x 13" pan.

2 Beat powdered sugar, cream cheese, and remaining 3 eggs at medium speed of an electric beater until creamy. Spoon powdered sugar mixture over batter in pan.

3 Bake at 300° for 1 hour. Cool and cut into 2½" to 3" squares. Serve with ice cream or whipped topping.

MEALTIME ✕ MATTERS

Family Time—After the dessert's been served, suggest a nice evening stroll for the entire family. It's a super way to unwind—and exercise—after a great meal together. If the weather isn't cooperating, gather the family for a board game, or better yet—have dessert while playing!

Chocolate Chip Pound Cake

12 to 14 servings

1   (18.25-ounce) package yellow cake
    mix (without pudding)
1   (5.9-ounce) package chocolate
    instant pudding mix
½   cup sugar
⅔   cup water
¾   cup vegetable oil

1   (8-ounce) container sour cream
4   large eggs
6   ounces mini semisweet chocolate
    chips

Powdered sugar

1 Preheat the oven to 350°. Beat first 5 ingredients in a large mixing bowl at medium speed of an electric beater about 2 minutes or until creamy.

2 Add sour cream, mixing well. Add eggs, 1 at a time, mixing at low speed just until blended after each addition. Stir in chocolate chips. Pour batter into a greased and floured 12-cup Bundt pan or 10" tube pan.

3 Bake at 350° for 1 hour or until a wooden toothpick inserted in center comes out clean. Cool in pan on a wire rack 10 minutes; remove from pan, and cool completely on wire rack. Sprinkle with powdered sugar before serving.

MEALTIME MATTERS

Edible Birthday Surprise—Having a birthday in the family? Place *edible* fresh flowers on top of an otherwise plain cake to make a pretty birthday cake. Use edible flowers from your yard, such as pansies, nasturtiums, marigolds, or violets, that you know haven't been treated with pesticides.

Easy Perfect Chocolate Cake

(pictured on page 4)

14 to 16 servings

1 (18.25-ounce) package devil's food
   cake mix with pudding
3 large eggs
1¼ cups water
½ cup vegetable oil

1 cup frozen whipped topping,
   thawed
Creamy Chocolate Frosting (see recipe
   below) or 2 (16-ounce) containers
   chocolate frosting
Chocolate-covered toffee candy bars,
   chopped

1 Preheat the oven to 350°. Beat first 4 ingredients at medium speed of an electric beater 2 minutes. Pour batter into 2 greased and floured 9" round cakepans.

2 Bake at 350° for 25 minutes or until a wooden toothpick inserted in center comes out clean. Cool in pans on wire racks 10 minutes; remove from pans, and cool completely on wire racks. Cover and chill 1 hour.

3 Spread whipped topping between layers. Spread Creamy Chocolate Frosting on top and sides of cake. Sprinkle with chopped candy bars. Serve immediately, or store in refrigerator.

Creamy Chocolate Frosting

1 cup (6 ounces) semisweet chocolate
   chips
½ cup half-and-half
1 cup butter
2½ cups powdered sugar

1 Cook first 3 ingredients in a heavy saucepan over medium heat, stirring until chocolate melts. Remove from heat; cool 15 minutes. Stir in powdered sugar.

2 Place pan in ice, and beat at medium speed of an electric beater about 8 minutes or until spreading consistency. Yield: 3 cups.

Shortcut Carrot Cake

(pictured on facing page)

14 to 16 servings

1   (26.5-ounce) package cinnamon
       streusel coffee cake mix, streusel
       and glaze packets reserved
3   large eggs
1¼ cups water
⅓   cup vegetable oil
3   large carrots, peeled and finely grated
1½ cups chopped pecans, toasted and
       divided
1   cup flaked coconut
2   tablespoons orange juice

Cream Cheese Frosting (see recipe
       below) or 2 (16-ounce) containers
       cream cheese frosting

1 Preheat the oven to 350°. Grease 3 (8") round cakepans. Line with parchment paper or wax paper.

2 Combine cake mix and streusel packet in a mixing bowl. Add eggs, water, and oil; beat at medium speed of an electric beater 2 minutes. Stir in carrots, ½ cup pecans, and the coconut. Pour batter evenly into prepared pans. Bake at 350° for 20 to 22 minutes. Cool in pans on wire racks 10 minutes. Invert pans onto racks; remove pans and paper. Stir together glaze packet and orange juice; brush over warm cake layers. Cool completely.

3 Spread frosting between layers and on top and sides of cake. Sprinkle sides of cake with remaining 1 cup pecans. Chill at least 2 hours.

Cream Cheese Frosting
1   (8-ounce) package cream cheese,
       softened
1   (3-ounce) package cream cheese,
       softened
¼   cup butter, softened
6   cups powdered sugar
2   teaspoons vanilla extract
1   to 2 teaspoons milk

1 Beat cream cheese and butter at medium speed of an electric beater until fluffy; gradually add powdered sugar, beating well. Stir in vanilla. Add milk, 1 teaspoon at a time, until spreading consistency. Yield: 4 cups.

Easy Oatmeal Cookies,
page 188

Fudge Balls,
page 201

Easy Strawberry Pie

(pictured on facing page)

6 to 8 servings

1   cup sugar
1   cup water
3   tablespoons cornstarch
¼   cup strawberry gelatin

5   cups fresh strawberries, halved
1   baked (9") pie crust
Sweetened whipped cream or frozen
       whipped topping, thawed
       (optional)

1 Bring first 3 ingredients to a boil in a saucepan over medium heat, and cook, stirring constantly, 1 minute or until thickened. Stir in gelatin until dissolved. Remove from heat; let cool to room temperature.

2 Arrange strawberries in pie crust, and pour gelatin mixture over strawberries. Cover and chill 2 hours. Serve pie with whipped cream, if desired.

Impressive Finale
This simple, classic treat is impressive enough to rival any restaurant dessert offering.

Refrigerator Blueberry Pie

6 to 8 servings

4   cups fresh blueberries, divided
1   cup sugar
¾   cup hot water
2   tablespoons cornstarch
¼   teaspoon salt
¼   teaspoon ground cinnamon

2   tablespoons lemon juice
1   baked 9" pie crust
Sweetened whipped cream

1 Combine 1 cup blueberries, the sugar, and next 4 ingredients in a saucepan. Cook over medium-high heat until mixture thickens, stirring constantly.

2 Add remaining 3 cups blueberries and the lemon juice; stir gently. Spoon into pie crust; cover and chill 1 hour or until set. Serve pie with sweetened whipped cream.

MEALTIME MATTERS

Coffee Talk—Want to "perk" up plain coffee? Add a cinnamon stick or vanilla bean to the coffeemaker basket. Stand by for fantastic flavor and aroma!

Coconut Cream Pie

6 to 8 servings

1⅔ cups graham cracker crumbs
¼ cup sugar
⅓ cup butter, melted

1 (8-ounce) package cream cheese, softened
1 cup cream of coconut (see tip)
1 (3.4-ounce) package cheesecake instant pudding mix
1 (6-ounce) package frozen sweetened flaked coconut, thawed
1 (8-ounce) container frozen whipped topping, thawed

1 cup whipping cream

1 Preheat the oven to 350°. Stir together first 3 ingredients; press mixture into bottom and up sides of a 9" pie plate. Bake at 350° for 8 minutes; remove to a wire rack, and cool completely.

2 Beat cream cheese and cream of coconut at medium speed of an electric beater until smooth. Add pudding mix, beating until blended. Stir in coconut; fold in whipped topping. Spread cheese mixture evenly into prepared crust; cover and chill 2 hours or until set.

3 Beat whipping cream with an electric beater until soft peaks form; spread evenly over pie.

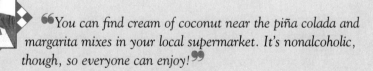

"You can find cream of coconut near the piña colada and margarita mixes in your local supermarket. It's nonalcoholic, though, so everyone can enjoy!"

Pumpkin Sundae Pie

6 to 8 servings

1¼ cups sugar
1 cup canned pumpkin
1 teaspoon pumpkin pie spice
½ teaspoon salt
1 cup whipping cream, whipped

3 cups vanilla ice cream, softened
1 baked 9" pie crust
Butterscotch Sauce (see recipe below)

1 Stir together first 4 ingredients in a large bowl; fold in whipped cream.

2 Spoon ice cream into pie crust, and spread evenly. Spoon pumpkin mixture over ice cream. Cover and freeze at least 3 hours. Serve with warm Butterscotch Sauce.

Butterscotch Sauce

1 cup packed light brown sugar
½ cup light corn syrup
½ cup water
1 teaspoon vanilla extract

1 Stir together first 3 ingredients in a saucepan; bring to a boil. Cook, uncovered, 5 minutes. Remove from heat; stir in vanilla. Yield: about 1 cup.

"Homemade butterscotch sauce tops off this frozen delight of ice cream layered with pumpkin, but if time is tight, commercial ice cream topping works, too. Be sure to follow the directions for heating the sauce."

Graham Cracker-Nut Torte

6 to 8 servings

3   large eggs, separated
1   cup graham cracker crumbs
1   cup packed brown sugar
1   teaspoon baking powder
¼   teaspoon salt
½   teaspoon vanilla extract
½   cup chopped pecans

Sweetened whipped cream (optional)

1 Preheat the oven to 350°. Combine egg yolks and next 6 ingredients, stirring well.

2 Beat egg whites at high speed of an electric beater until stiff peaks form; fold into crumb mixture. Spoon into a greased and floured 9" pie plate.

3 Bake at 350° for 25 to 30 minutes or until golden. Serve torte warm or cold with sweetened whipped cream, if desired.

"This brownielike torte will stick to the pie plate, so don't try to turn it out onto a cake plate. Just spoon it up and take individual servings to the table."

Creamy Lemon Tartlets

15 tartlets

1 (2.1-ounce) package frozen mini phyllo pastry shells

⅓ cup lemon curd (see tip on page 150)
½ cup whipping cream
¼ teaspoon almond extract
Fresh mint leaves (optional)

1 Bake pastry shells according to package directions; cool completely.

2 Beat lemon curd, whipping cream, and almond extract at medium speed of an electric beater until thickened and soft peaks form. Spoon into baked pastry shells. Chill tartlets 1 hour. Garnish with fresh mint leaves, if desired.

More the Merrier!

Mix things up a bit! If you're having a crowd, try these tartlets with orange or strawberry curd, too. Or why not serve all 3 flavors at once? Just prepare the recipe 3 times, each time using a different flavored curd.

Cookie Jar Jubilee

"Dip your hand into my cookie jar to discover a vast selection of yummy homemade cookies and candies."

Cake Mix Cookies

about 5 dozen

1   (18.25-ounce) package devil's food
      cake mix
1   large egg
½   (8-ounce) container frozen whipped
      topping, thawed

½   cup sifted powdered sugar

1 Preheat the oven to 350°. Combine first 3 ingredients, stirring well. (Dough will be sticky.)

2 Dust hands with powdered sugar, and shape dough into ¾" balls. Coat balls with powdered sugar, and place 2" apart on ungreased baking sheets.

3 Bake at 350° for 10 to 12 minutes or until done; remove cookies to wire racks to cool.

❝Thanks to cake mix, these homemade cookies are almost effortless. What are you waiting for? Tear open a package and reap the rewards!❞

Double Chocolate Cookies
about 4½ dozen

1   (18.25-ounce) package chocolate
      cake mix
½   cup vegetable oil
2   large eggs

1   cup (6 ounces) semisweet chocolate
      chips
½   cup chopped pecans

1 Preheat the oven to 350°. Beat first 3 ingredients at medium speed of an electric beater until batter is smooth.

2 Stir in chocolate chips and pecans. Drop by heaping teaspoonfuls onto ungreased baking sheets.

3 Bake at 350° for 8 to 10 minutes. Remove to wire racks to cool.

MEALTIME MATTERS

Rainy Day Fun—Involve the kids in some kitchen fun if inclement weather keeps them indoors. Helping hands are always appreciated—especially for cookie making! With this easy recipe and Mom's supervision, you'll have double chocolaty rewards within 15 minutes—start to finish!

Chocolaty Oatmeal Drops

about 5½ dozen

1 cup (6 ounces) semisweet chocolate
  chips, divided
1 (22.3-ounce) package sugar
  cookie mix
1 cup uncooked quick-cooking oats
⅓ cup vegetable oil
1 teaspoon water
1 teaspoon vanilla extract
2 large eggs, lightly beaten

1 Preheat the oven to 350°. Melt ½ cup chocolate chips in a saucepan over low heat, stirring often. Combine melted chocolate, sugar cookie mix, and remaining 5 ingredients in a large bowl, stirring until well blended. Stir in remaining ½ cup chocolate chips.

2 Drop dough by heaping teaspoonfuls 1" apart onto lightly greased baking sheets. Bake at 350° for 10 minutes. Let cool slightly; remove to wire racks, and let cool completely.

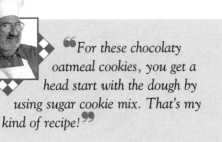

"For these chocolaty oatmeal cookies, you get a head start with the dough by using sugar cookie mix. That's my kind of recipe!"

Heavenly Chocolate-Chip Meringue Cookies

about 30 cookies

2   egg whites
¼   teaspoon cream of tartar
⅔   cup sugar
½   cup (3 ounces) mini semisweet
        chocolate chips

1 Preheat the oven to 400°. Beat egg whites and cream of tartar at high speed of an electric beater 1 minute or until soft peaks form. Gradually add sugar to egg white mixture, beating 2½ minutes or until stiff peaks form and sugar dissolves. Gently fold in chocolate chips.

2 Drop by teaspoonfuls onto 2 lightly greased parchment paper-lined baking sheets.

3 Place in 400° oven, and turn oven off. Leave in oven 8 hours or overnight.

"These melt-in-your-mouth cookies are ooh-so-easy to make. Prepare 'em in the evening and then put 'em in the oven, and forget about 'em 'til the next morning! Ooh! What a heavenly treat to wake up to!"

Easy Oatmeal Cookies

(pictured on page 174)

about 3½ dozen

1   (18.25-ounce) package yellow
       cake mix
2   cups uncooked quick-cooking oats
1   cup sugar
1   cup vegetable oil
2   large eggs
1   cup chopped pecans
1½   teaspoons vanilla extract

1 Preheat the oven to 350°. Combine first 3 ingredients in a large bowl. Combine oil and eggs; add to dry ingredients, stirring well. Stir in pecans and vanilla.

2 Drop dough by rounded tablespoonfuls 2" apart onto ungreased baking sheets.

3 Bake at 350° for 12 minutes or until lightly browned. Let cool in pan 2 minutes. Carefully remove to wire racks to cool.

MEALTIME ✕ MATTERS

Cookie Swap—Instead of slaving in the kitchen during the holidays making batches of lots of different cookies, plan a cookie swap with your best buds. Have each person bake their family favorite—a dozen or more per person that's invited plus extras to munch on. Then everyone will get to take a variety of cookies home to share with the rest of the family. Don't forget to include your recipe!

Turtle Cookies

about 20 cookies

2 cups all-purpose flour
1 cup packed brown sugar
½ cup butter, softened
1 cup pecan halves

⅔ cup butter
½ cup packed brown sugar

1 cup milk chocolate chips

1 Preheat the oven to 350°. Combine first 3 ingredients in a mixing bowl; beat well at medium speed of an electric beater. Pat mixture firmly into an ungreased 9" x 13" pan. Arrange pecans over crust.

2 Combine ⅔ cup butter and ½ cup brown sugar in a saucepan. Bring to a boil over medium heat, stirring constantly; boil 3 minutes, stirring constantly. Spoon mixture over pecans. Bake at 350° for 15 to 17 minutes or until golden and bubbly.

3 Remove from oven; sprinkle top with chocolate chips. Let stand 2 to 3 minutes or until slightly melted. Gently swirl chocolate with a knife, leaving some chips whole (do not spread); let cool. Cut into squares.

MEALTIME MATTERS

It's a Wrap!—Be creative when packaging homemade cookies and candies for gift giving. Use colorful tins, bags, boxes, or cellophane to add a decorative and festive touch to your package. And don't forget a special gift tag and note. These added touches will be a reminder of your gift long after the goodies are gone.

Wedding Cookies

about 4 dozen

½ cup butter, softened
1 cup all-purpose flour
¼ cup sugar
1 teaspoon vanilla extract
1 cup finely chopped pecans

1 cup powdered sugar

1 Preheat the oven to 400°. Beat butter at medium speed of an electric beater until creamy. Add flour, sugar, and vanilla, beating until blended. Stir in pecans. (Dough will be stiff.) Shape into 1" balls, and place on ungreased baking sheets.

2 Bake at 400° for 10 minutes. Remove to wire racks, and cool slightly. Roll warm cookies in powdered sugar, and cool completely on wire racks.

"Mama would make these small, round buttery cookies when she'd have the gals over—they're a cinch to make! You may have heard 'em referred to as Mexican wedding cakes or Russian tea cakes—many cultures have their own rendition of this rich cookie."

Elephant Ears

about 8 servings

1   cup sugar
¼   cup ground cinnamon
1   (10-ounce) can refrigerated
       cinnamon rolls

1 Preheat the oven to 375°. Combine sugar and cinnamon in a small bowl. Remove rolls from can; set icing aside. Sprinkle rolls with sugar mixture, and roll each into a 6" round. Sprinkle rolls with sugar mixture again.

2 Place rolls on lightly greased baking sheets. Bake at 375° for 7 minutes. Cool slightly on baking sheets; drizzle reserved icing over hot rolls, if desired.

"These crispy pastries get their unusual name from their size and appearance. When rolled and baked, they resemble elephant ears! Make them extra sweet by drizzling icing over the hot rolls."

Angel Fluff Brownies

about 16 brownies

1   (3.3-ounce) package chocolate
        instant pudding mix
⅔   cup sugar
½   cup all-purpose flour
2   large eggs
⅓   cup butter, melted
¼   cup whipping cream
1   teaspoon vanilla extract
½   cup chopped walnuts, toasted

Powdered sugar (optional)

1 Preheat the oven to 350°. Stir together the first 8 ingredients until blended. Spoon into a lightly greased 8" or 9" square pan.

2 Bake at 350° for 25 minutes or until edges pull away from pan. Cool in pan on a wire rack. Sprinkle with powdered sugar, if desired.

Your Choice

For fun and flavorful variations, pick your favorite pudding flavor. Just use it in place of the chocolate pudding, and proceed as directed.

Ooey Gooey Brownies

about 2 dozen

1	(21-ounce) package brownie mix
2	large eggs
¼	cup water
¼	cup vegetable oil
1	(8-ounce) container sour cream
2	cups (12 ounces) semisweet chocolate chips
1	cup chopped pecans

1 Preheat the oven to 350°. Combine first 4 ingredients; stir until well blended.

2 Stir in sour cream, chocolate chips, and pecans. Spoon into a greased 9" x 13" pan.

3 Bake at 350° for 32 to 35 minutes or until done; cool and cut into squares.

Instant Desserts

In a pinch for a quick dessert? Use leftover desserts for a new finale. Just layer crumbled leftover brownies—or cookies—with chocolate pudding and whipped topping in parfait glasses for a simple chocolate lover's specialty.

Pumpkin Cheesecake Squares

about 4 dozen

1 (16-ounce) package pound cake mix
4 teaspoons pumpkin pie spice, divided
3 large eggs
2 tablespoons butter, melted

1 (8-ounce) package cream cheese, softened
1 (15-ounce) can pumpkin
1 (14-ounce) can sweetened condensed milk
½ teaspoon salt
1 cup chopped pecans

1 Preheat the oven to 350°. Combine cake mix, 2 teaspoons pumpkin pie spice, 1 egg, and the melted butter in a large mixing bowl; beat at low speed of an electric beater until crumbly. Press dough into a greased 10" x 15" rimmed baking sheet.

2 Beat softened cream cheese at medium speed until creamy. Add remaining 2 teaspoons pumpkin pie spice, remaining 2 eggs, the pumpkin, condensed milk, and salt; beat until blended. Pour over crust; sprinkle with pecans.

3 Bake at 350° for 30 minutes or until set. Cool completely in pan on a wire rack. Cover and chill. Cut into squares.

" Pumpkin and spice make these squares perfect holiday fare, while a pound cake mix makes 'em a snap to prepare. "

No-Bake Granola Bars

about 4½ dozen

2½ cups crispy rice cereal
2 cups uncooked quick-cooking oats
½ cup raisins

½ cup packed brown sugar
½ cup light corn syrup
½ cup peanut butter
1 teaspoon vanilla extract

½ cup milk chocolate chips

1 Combine first 3 ingredients in a large bowl; set aside.

2 Bring brown sugar and corn syrup to a boil in a small saucepan over medium-high heat, stirring constantly; remove from heat. Stir in peanut butter and vanilla until blended.

3 Pour peanut butter mixture over cereal mixture, stirring until coated; let stand 10 minutes. Stir in chocolate chips. Press mixture into an ungreased 9" x 13" pan; cool in pan on a wire rack. Cut into bars.

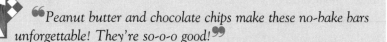

"Peanut butter and chocolate chips make these no-bake bars unforgettable! They're so-o-o good!"

Cookie-Ice Cream Bars

about 16 servings

1   cup chopped pecans
1   cup flaked coconut
2½ cups crispy rice cereal, crushed

1   cup packed light brown sugar
½   cup butter

1   quart vanilla ice cream, softened

Once these freeze, cut 'em into squares, and wrap 'em individually with plastic wrap for a ready-made treat. Kids of all ages will love 'em!

1 Preheat the oven to 350°. Bake pecans and coconut in a rimmed baking sheet at 350° for 5 to 10 minutes or until toasted, stirring occasionally. Combine pecans, coconut, and cereal in a bowl.

2 Bring brown sugar and butter to a boil in a small saucepan over medium heat, stirring constantly; boil 1 minute, stirring constantly. Pour sugar mixture over cereal mixture, stirring until coated.

3 Press half of cereal mixture into a 9" square pan lined with plastic wrap; freeze until firm. Spread with ice cream; press remaining cereal mixture over ice cream. Cover and freeze 8 hours or until firm. Cut into bars.

Triple Chocolate Clusters

about 6 dozen

2   (4-ounce) white chocolate bars
1   cup milk chocolate chips
1   cup (6 ounces) semisweet chocolate
      chips

1½ cups chopped peanuts
1½ cups broken pretzels

1 Melt first 3 ingredients in a heavy saucepan over low heat, stirring constantly.

2 Stir in peanuts and pretzels. Drop by tablespoonfuls onto lightly greased wax paper. Cool until hardened. Store in an airtight container in refrigerator.

"Three kinds of chocolate send these treats over the top! They're a cinch to make and can be stored up to a month in your fridge."

Cracker Candy

about 10 servings

2½ cups miniature round buttery
crackers

¾ cup butter
¾ cup packed brown sugar

2 cups milk chocolate chips
Chopped pecans (optional)
Rainbow candy sprinkles (optional)

1 Preheat the oven to 350°. Line a 9" x 13" pan with aluminum foil; then lightly coat foil with nonstick cooking spray, and add crackers.

2 Bring butter and brown sugar to a boil in a medium saucepan, stirring constantly; cook 3 minutes, stirring often. Pour mixture over crackers.

3 Bake at 350° for 5 minutes. Turn oven off. Sprinkle crackers with chocolate chips, and let stand in oven 3 minutes or until chocolate melts. Spread melted chocolate evenly over crackers. If desired, top with pecans and/or candy sprinkles. Cool and then break into pieces. Store in an airtight container in refrigerator.

"M-m-m! These chocolate confections are so easy to make and so sweet to eat. You better make extra 'cause they'll disappear in seconds!"

Pecan Clusters

about 12 dozen

1	(7-ounce) jar marshmallow creme
1½	pounds milk chocolate kisses
5	cups sugar
1	(12-ounce) can evaporated milk
½	cup butter
6	cups pecan halves

1 Place marshmallow creme and chocolate in a large bowl.

2 Bring sugar, milk, and butter to a boil in a large heavy saucepan, stirring constantly. Boil 8 minutes, stirring constantly. Add to marshmallow creme mixture, stirring until chocolate melts.

3 Stir in pecans. Drop by rounded teaspoonfuls onto wax paper-lined baking sheets; chill until firm. Store candy in refrigerator.

Handy-Dandy Candy Tips

• Read the recipe before you start—make sure you have all the ingredients on hand.
• Use a heavy-bottomed saucepan to prevent the candy from burning.
• Store layers of candy between sheets of wax paper in containers with tight-fitting lids.

Microwave Chocolate Fudge

about 3 dozen

3 cups milk chocolate chips
1 (14-ounce) can sweetened
  condensed milk
¼ cup butter, cut into pieces

1 Combine all ingredients in a microwave-safe 2-quart glass bowl. Microwave chocolate mixture at MEDIUM (50% power) 5 minutes, stirring at 1½-minute intervals. Pour into a greased 8" square dish. Cover and chill 8 hours; cut into 1½" squares. Store in refrigerator.

"No candy thermometer needed for this fudge—just your microwave and fridge! I recommend chilling the fudge about 8 hours so it can firm up nicely before you cut into it."

Fudge Balls

(pictured on page 175)

about 5 dozen

1½ pounds milk chocolate, broken into
   pieces
1   cup whipping cream

2   cups ground walnuts, toasted

1 Melt chocolate in a heavy saucepan over low heat, stirring until smooth. Meanwhile, beat whipping cream at medium speed of an electric beater until soft peaks form. Gradually add melted chocolate, and beat 15 minutes. Cover and chill 8 hours.

2 Working quickly, shape half of chocolate mixture into 1" balls. Place balls on a wax paper-lined rimmed baking sheet. (Keep remaining half of chocolate mixture chilled.) Repeat procedure with remaining chocolate mixture. Roll balls in walnuts until completely coated. Store in an airtight container in refrigerator.

Worth the Wait
The dough for this trufflelike candy needs to chill 8 hours, but the wait's worth it. Chilling the chocolate helps to make 'em velvety smooth, creamy—and yummy!

Praline Pecans

about 1 ½ cups

1 ½ cups chopped pecans
¼   cup packed light brown sugar
2   tablespoons whipping cream

1 Preheat the oven to 350°. Combine all ingredients; spread into a lightly buttered 9" round cakepan.

2 Bake at 350° for 20 minutes or until coating is slightly crystallized, stirring once. Remove from oven; stir and cool. Store in an airtight container.

Praline Almonds

Substitute 1 ½ cups chopped sliced blanched almonds for the pecans. Then bake at 350° for only 15 minutes, stirring once. Yield: about 1 ½ cups.

Coconut Scotchies

about 4 dozen

½ cup butter, softened
½ cup sugar
½ cup packed brown sugar
2 large eggs
1 teaspoon vanilla extract

2 cups all-purpose flour
½ teaspoon baking soda
1 cup butterscotch chips
½ cup chopped pecans

1½ cups flaked coconut

1 Preheat the oven to 350°. Beat butter at medium speed of an electric beater until creamy; gradually add sugars, beating well. Add eggs and vanilla; beat well.

2 Combine flour and soda; add to butter mixture, and beat well. Stir in butterscotch chips and pecans.

3 Place coconut in a shallow dish. Drop dough by rounded teaspoonfuls into coconut, rolling to coat dough with coconut while shaping dough into balls. Place balls on greased baking sheets. Bake at 350° for 10 minutes. Immediately remove to wire racks to cool.

Smart Cookies

• Lightly grease baking sheets only if the recipe specifies, using nonstick cooking spray or solid vegetable shortening. Butter encourages burning.
• Use a dinnerware teaspoon—not a measuring spoon—to scoop cookie dough.
• Bake one batch at a time on the middle oven rack. If you need to bake more than one batch at the same time, be sure to rotate the baking sheets from top to bottom rack halfway through the cooking time.
• Allow your baking sheets to cool completely between batches before reuse.

METRIC EQUIVALENTS

The recipes that appear in this cookbook use the standard United States method for measuring liquid and dry or solid ingredients (teaspoons, tablespoons, and cups). The information in the following charts is provided to help cooks outside the U.S. successfully use these recipes. All equivalents are approximate.

EQUIVALENTS FOR DIFFERENT TYPES OF INGREDIENTS

A standard cup measure of a dry or solid ingredient will vary in weight depending on the type of ingredient. A standard cup of liquid is the same volume for any type of liquid. Use the following chart when converting standard cup measures to grams (weight) or milliliters (volume).

Standard Cup	Fine Powder (ex. flour)	Grain (ex. rice)	Granular (ex. sugar)	Liquid Solids (ex. butter)	Liquid (ex. milk)
1	140 g	150 g	190 g	200 g	240 ml
¾	105 g	113 g	143 g	150 g	180 ml
⅔	93 g	100 g	125 g	133 g	160 ml
½	70 g	75 g	95 g	100 g	120 ml
⅓	47 g	50 g	63 g	67 g	80 ml
¼	35 g	38 g	48 g	50 g	60 ml
⅛	18 g	19 g	24 g	25 g	30 ml

DRY INGREDIENTS BY WEIGHT

(To convert ounces to grams, multiply the number of ounces by 30.)

1 oz	=	¹⁄₁₆ lb	=	30 g
4 oz	=	¼ lb	=	120 g
8 oz	=	½ lb	=	240 g
12 oz	=	¾ lb	=	360 g
16 oz	=	1 lb	=	480 g

LENGTH

(To convert inches to centimeters, multiply the number of inches by 2.5.)

1 in			=	2.5 cm		
6 in	=	½ ft	=	15 cm		
12 in	=	1 ft	=	30 cm		
36 in	=	3 ft	= 1 yd	=	90 cm		
40 in			=	100 cm	=	1 meter

LIQUID INGREDIENTS BY VOLUME

¼ tsp					=	1 ml		
½ tsp					=	2 ml		
1 tsp					=	5 ml		
3 tsp	=	1 tbls			=	½ fl oz	=	15 ml
		2 tbls	=	⅛ cup	=	1 fl oz	=	30 ml
		4 tbls	=	¼ cup	=	2 fl oz	=	60 ml
		5⅓ tbls	=	⅓ cup	=	3 fl oz	=	80 ml
		8 tbls	=	½ cup	=	4 fl oz	=	120 ml
		10⅔ tbls	=	⅔ cup	=	5 fl oz	=	160 ml
		12 tbls	=	¾ cup	=	6 fl oz	=	180 ml
		16 tbls	=	1 cup	=	8 fl oz	=	240 ml
		1 pt	=	2 cups	=	16 fl oz	=	480 ml
		1 qt	=	4 cups	=	32 fl oz	=	960 ml
						33 fl oz	= 1000 ml	= 1 liter

COOKING/OVEN TEMPERATURES

	Fahrenheit	Celsius	Gas Mark
Freeze Water	32° F	0° C	
Room Temperature	68° F	20° C	
Boil Water	212° F	100° C	
Bake	325° F	160° C	3
	350° F	180° C	4
	375° F	190° C	5
	400° F	200° C	6
	425° F	220° C	7
	450° F	230° C	8
Broil	Broil	Broil	Grill

Index

FAVORITE RECIPES

Jot down the family's and your favorite recipes here for handy-dandy, fast reference.
And don't forget to include the dishes that drew oohs and aahs when you had the gang over.

Recipe	Source/Page	Remarks